THE TRUTH ABOUT

Heaven

**WHAT THE BIBLE SAYS
ABOUT LIFE AFTER DEATH**

TIME HOME ENTERTAINMENT

PUBLISHER Jim Childs
VICE PRESIDENT AND ASSOCIATE PUBLISHER Margot Schupf
VICE PRESIDENT, FINANCE Vandana Patel
EXECUTIVE DIRECTOR, MARKETING SERVICES Carol Pittard
EXECUTIVE DIRECTOR, BUSINESS DEVELOPMENT Suzanne Albert
EXECUTIVE DIRECTOR, MARKETING Susan Hettleman
PUBLISHING DIRECTOR Megan Pearlman
ASSOCIATE DIRECTOR OF PUBLICITY Courtney Greenhalgh
ASSOCIATE GENERAL COUNSEL Simone Procas
ASSISTANT DIRECTOR, SPECIAL SALES Ilene Schreider
**SENIOR MANAGER, BUSINESS DEVELOPMENT
AND PARTNERSHIPS** Nina Fleishman Reed
EDITOR, BRAND DEVELOPMENT Katie McHugh Malm
ASSOCIATE PRODUCTION MANAGER Kimberly Marshall
ASSOCIATE PREPRESS MANAGER Alex Voznesenskiy
ASSISTANT PROJECT MANAGER Hillary Hirsch

EDITORIAL DIRECTOR Stephen Koepp
SENIOR EDITOR Roe D'Angelo
COPY CHIEF Rina Bander
DESIGN MANAGER Anne-Michelle Gallero
EDITORIAL OPERATIONS Gina Scauzillo

GENERAL EDITOR
Christopher D. Hudson

WRITERS
Randy Southern
Selena Sarns
Christopher D. Hudson
Sammy Thale

DESIGN AND PRODUCTION
Mark Wainwright, Symbology Creative

Special Thanks: Katherine Barnet, Brad Beatson, Jeremy Biloon, Susan Chodakiewicz, Rose Cirrincione, Assu Etsubneh, Christine Font, Susan Hettleman, David Kahn, Jean Kennedy, Amy Mangus, Nina Mistry, Dave Rozzelle, Matthew Ryan, Ricardo Santiago, Holly Smith, Adriana Tierno

ISBN 10: 1-61893-354-X
ISBN 13: 978-1-61893-354-6

We welcome your comments and suggestions about Time Home Entertainment Books. Please write to us at:
Time Home Entertainment Books
Attention: Book Editors
PO Box 11016
Des Moines, IA 50336-1016

If you would like to order any of our hardcover Collector's Edition books, please call us at 1-800-327-6388, Monday through Friday, 7 a.m. to 8 p.m., or Saturday, 7 a.m. to 6 p.m., Central Time.

ART SOURCES
Shutterstock, Thinkstock, iStock, Art Resource, Wikipedia

QUOTES
p21   Helen Keller, *The Story of My Life* (Grosset & Dunlap, 1905), 111.
p58   Randy Alcorn, *Heaven* (Tyndale House Publishers, 2011), 16.
p65   Dwight L. Moody, *Heaven* (Moody Publishers, 1995), 103.
p71   J. I. Packer, "Dr. J. I. Packer Answers the Question 'Will A Loving God Really Condemn People to Hell?'" LifeCoach4God, August 16, 2013, http://verticallivingministries.com/2012/04/09/dr-j-i-packer-answers-the-question-will-a-loving-god-really-condemn-people-to-hell/.
p93   Mark Driscoll, "To Hell with Hell?" *Resurgence: A Ministry of Mars Hill Church*, August 16, 2013
p100 Rick Warren, *The Purpose Driven Life: What on Earth Am I Here For?* (Grand Rapids: Zondervan, 2002), 47–50.
p120 H. G. Wells, *A Short History of the World* (Princeton University: Macmillan Company, 1922), 215.
p138 Dave Earley, *The 21 Most Amazing Truths About Heaven* (Uhrichsville, OH: Barbour Publishing, 2006), 159–160.
p143 Tony Evans, *Tony Evans Speaks Out on Heaven and Hell* (Chicago, IL: Moody Publishers, 2000), 11–14.
p149 Paul P. Enns, *Heaven Revealed: What Is It Like? What Will We Do? . . . And 11 Other Things You've Wondered About* (Chicago: Moody Publishers, 2011), 35–38.
p166 C. S. Lewis, *Mere Christianity* (Simon & Schuster, Limited, 1996), 147–148.
p177 Mitch Albom, *The Five People You Meet in Heaven* (Hyperion, 2006), 35.

INTRODUCTION

The thought of life after death can be both fascinating and terrifying.

No matter our faith background, we all wonder what might happen after we die: *Where exactly are heaven and hell, and what are they like? How do we get there? What exactly will we do for all eternity? Who will be with us in the afterlife? Will we see our childhood pets in heaven? Don't only really bad people go to hell? What will we look like in heaven?*

Although finding answers to these questions is a challenge, one source has stood the test of time and provided hope, comfort, and reliable information for thousands of years: the Bible.

The Truth about Heaven outlines many details and provides answers to some of the most common questions people have about heaven and the afterlife. Relying solely on the information provided in the Bible, we've collected inspiring and challenging insights about life after death.

Rather than defend a cause or argue a theological framework, we've maintained a conservative point of view by allowing the Bible to speak for itself. No key details have been omitted for the sake of brevity or easier comprehension. Passages that seem to cast the depths of hell as a negative reality have been left intact. We've been careful not to rewrite what the Bible says but to clearly present what it teaches.

Our hope is simply that you might better know the truth about heaven as it is presented in God's Word.

Christopher D. Hudson, Editor
Facebook.com/Christopher.D.Hudson.books
Twitter.com/ReadEngageApply

TABLE OF CONTENTS

CH. 4   The Path To Heaven and Hell

CH. 5   Heavenly Questions

Ask the question, "What is heaven to you?" and you are bound to get a variety of answers.

Heaven is a week in Barbados, Christmas with my family, or a long soak in a hot tub after a hard day.

Like heaven, hell can be defined in ultrapersonal ways. The French philosopher Jean-Paul Sartre famously said, "Hell is other people." The "other people" in question certainly have ideas of their own.

To wit, hell is French philosophy, rush-hour traffic, or a day-long webinar.

But when the topic turns to the heaven and hell of Christian theology—and to references in Scripture of the hereafter—consensus can be just as difficult to find, even among believers. Though the Bible has plenty to say about life after death, some of its fantastic descriptions lend themselves to different interpretations, to say the least.

CHAPTER 1

WHAT DO YOU MEAN BY "HEAVEN" AND "HELL"?

In this section, we will look at some of the "big-picture" issues concerning the hereafter, including the following:

- Where heaven is found and what it looks like
- How Christians will experience heaven
- What impact sin will have in heaven
- What rewards await believers
- Whether the concept of purgatory is biblically supported

- Where hell is found
- How people will experience hell
- What individual consequences await people in hell
- Whether hell will exist forever

We may not find consensus, but we can find a starting point in our discussion of life after death.

HEAVEN: SO CLOSE, YET SO FAR AWAY

Field of Dreams was named one of the best-loved movies of the past quarter century. The film's popularity was due, in part, to its hopeful depiction of the afterlife and the possibility of reuniting with loved ones who have passed away. A running joke in the movie begins when one of the long-dead ball players, inexplicably emerging from a cornfield to play on a "magical" baseball diamond, asks, "Is this heaven?"

The reply: "No, it's Iowa."

The Bible does not give us precise coordinates for the location of heaven, but we can be pretty sure of one thing: it won't be mistaken for Iowa.

Location, in fact, is a loaded word in discussions of the afterlife. Many people believe heaven is not a location, per se, but a spiritual state of being. Others believe heaven is a reaction to being in God's presence. That is to say, everyone enters God's presence after death. For those who love him, it will be heaven; for those who don't, it will be hell.

The Bible, however, speaks of heaven as a destination—a place. In fact, it speaks of three heavens. The first heaven is located in the outer reaches of the earth's atmosphere, where clouds and birds are found. *"The LORD will open the storehouses of the skies where he keeps the rain, and he will send rain on your land at just the right times. He will make you successful in everything you do"* (Deuteronomy 28:12).

The second heaven is outer space, where the sun, moon, and planets are found. *"Light will disappear from the stars in the sky; the dawning sun will turn dark, and the moon will lose its brightness"* (Isaiah 13:10).

The third heaven is God's dwelling place—the location of his throne. *"I am your servant, and the people of Israel belong to you. So whenever any of us look toward this temple and pray, answer from your home in heaven and forgive our sins"* (1 Kings 8:30).

This is the heaven the apostle Paul reported visiting. *"I know about one of Christ's followers who was taken up into the third heaven 14 years ago. I don't know if the man was still in his body when it happened, but God certainly knows. As I said, only God really knows if this man was in his body at the time. But he was taken up into paradise, where he heard things too wonderful to tell"* (2 Corinthians 12:2–4).

The progressive distance from the earth to the three heavens (like concentric circles on a bull's-eye target) has led some to speculate that heaven lies beyond the outer edges of space. Yet heaven is where God's presence is—and God's presence is never far from his people. Stephen, the first-known Christian martyr, saw heaven clearly just before he died (Acts 7:55–56).

These tantalizing, yet seemingly contradictory, clues make heaven the rarest of anomalies in our GPS-centric culture—a place unfindable by modern technology, yet eminently accessible to all.

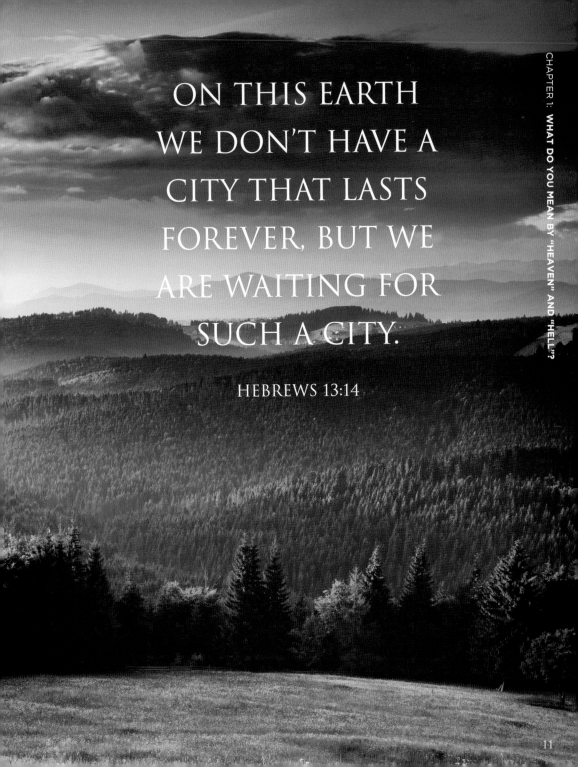

ON THIS EARTH
WE DON'T HAVE A
CITY THAT LASTS
FOREVER, BUT WE
ARE WAITING FOR
SUCH A CITY.

HEBREWS 13:14

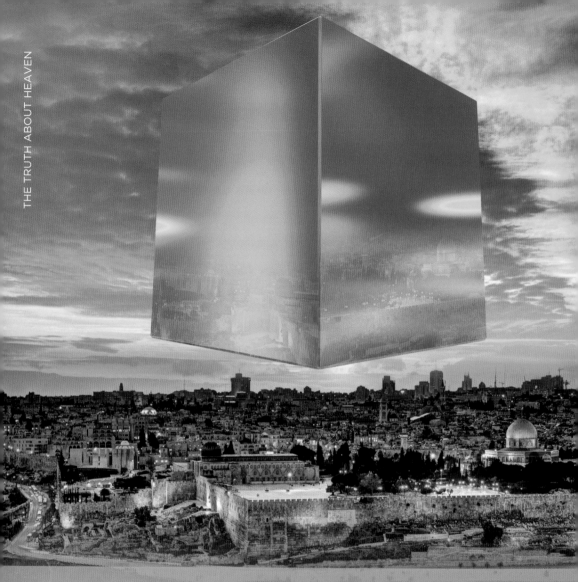

Read It for Yourself
REVELATION 21:9–14

I saw one of the seven angels who had the bowls filled with the seven last terrible troubles. The angel came to me and said, "Come on! I will show you the one who will be the bride and wife of the Lamb." Then with the help of the Spirit, he took me to the top of a very high mountain. There he showed me the holy city of Jerusalem coming down from God in heaven.

A PLACE LIKE NO OTHER

Pity the poor apostle John. The man had no formal education to speak of, no literary or religious training. For crying out loud, he made his living as a fisherman. Nothing in his background or experience prepared him for the task he was assigned in AD 95.

That's the year God tapped him and gave him a vision of things to come—which included a private tour of heaven itself. The scope of John's access to "all things eternal" was unprecedented. No one this side of the afterlife had ever explored heaven as extensively as John did.

He was given a unique opportunity and responsibility. John was charged with writing down the things he saw in his vision for posterity in what would become the New Testament book of Revelation. The vast majority of what Christians believe about heaven, the future, and eternity comes from John.

It's no insult to the man to suggest that parts of his narrative are just as confusing as they are provocative. Perhaps no writer could have done justice to the sights John was privy to. What he left us to wrangle with are descriptions of an utterly unique place—quite unlike anywhere else:

- A city made of pure gold, as clear as glass, and shaped like a perfect cube of equal distance (about 1,500 miles) in length, width, and height
- A wall, 216-feet thick, made of jasper and built on a foundation of twelve precious stones
- Twelve gates, each one made of a single pearl
- A source of illumination—God himself—so bright that no sun or moon is needed
- A river flowing with the crystal-clear water of life that originates from God's throne

Faced with a near-impossible literary challenge, John drew on familiar images to describe the things he was seeing. Part of the fun of heaven will be matching John's fantastic descriptions to their actual heavenly counterparts. Until then, we have his words to draw from as we form our own mental images of the uniqueness of our heavenly home.

The glory of God made the city bright. It was dazzling and crystal clear like a precious jasper stone. The city had a high and thick wall with twelve gates, and each one of them was guarded by an angel. On each of the gates was written the name of one of the twelve tribes of Israel. Three of these gates were on the east, three were on the north, three more were on the south, and the other three were on the west. The city was built on twelve foundation stones. On each of the stones was written the name of one of the Lamb's twelve apostles.

The dimensions of heaven stagger the imagination. In the midst of the apostle John's vision, a helpful angel with a gold measuring stick revealed some of the raw numbers. New Jerusalem—the city that descends from heaven as the eternal dwelling place of God's people—is said to be approximately 1,500 miles long, 1,500 miles wide, and 1,500 miles high (Revelation 21:16). We're talking about a total area of *billions* of miles. For comparison's sake, New York City covers approximately 468 square miles.

As for the population, who can say? How many people in human history have put their faith in Jesus? How many angels did God create? How many other "as yet unidentified" beings occupy heaven? Billions? Trillions? Quadrillions? More?

The numbers can boggle the mind and give slight pause to the heaven bound. After all, in the face of such enormity, how can we not feel a bit overwhelmed? Won't we feel disoriented in a place more expansive than we can possibly imagine? Will we become just another face in an endless crowd?

Two Bible passages offer us clues. The first is Hebrews 13:14: *"On this earth we don't have a city that lasts forever, but we are waiting for such a city."* Think of the place in this world that feels most like home—the place where you feel most comfortable, most secure, most loved, most welcomed.

Heaven will surpass it.

Dimensions aside, heaven will feel like home. We were created specifically to dwell there, in God's presence. Our sense of belonging, of being where we are meant to be, will be more profound there than anywhere else on earth.

The second passage is John 14:2: *"There are many rooms in my Father's house. I wouldn't tell you this, unless it was true. I am going there to prepare a place for each of you."*

The operative words here are "for you." Jesus knows us better than our closest friends do. He knows—and wants—what will bring us ultimate joy and fulfillment. And in heaven, he will make it happen. Heaven will have an unmistakable personal touch for us, thanks to Jesus, our *personal* Savior.

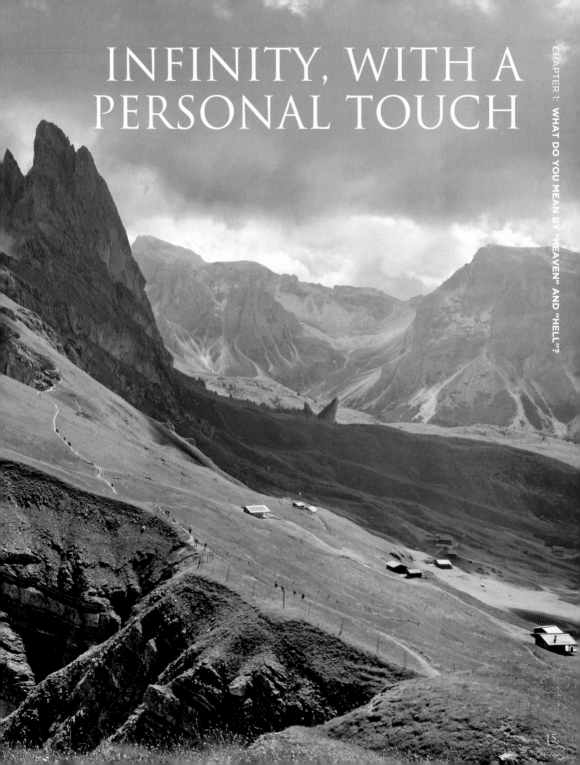

INFINITY, WITH A PERSONAL TOUCH

A WORKER'S PARADISE

Every so often in pop culture, heaven is portrayed as an eternal vacation, a place to relax forever after a lifetime of work and service on earth. Truth be told, such a place would more closely resemble hell than heaven.

We were designed for work—to find fulfillment and satisfaction in labor. In God's plan for creation (see chapter 4), work was a key element of life, as exemplified in the Garden of Eden.

Then came sin and the fall of humankind. Everything changed as a result of God's curse, *including* the nature of work. What was once fulfilling became difficult and unpleasant. Generally speaking, work no longer energized us. In fact, it drained us.

In heaven, though, work will be restored to its former celebrated position. *"God's curse will no longer be on the people of that city. He and the Lamb will be seated there on their thrones, and its people will worship God. . . . Never again will night appear, and no one who lives there will ever need a lamp or the sun. The Lord God will be their light, and they will rule forever"* (Revelation 22:3, 5).

God's people are his servants who serve him. That is to say, they work for God. Likewise, to "rule" (or reign) is to work. Heaven is a place where work is done. We're not talking about menial labor here. We're not talking about punching in and then counting the hours until we can punch out. We're not talking about soul-crushingly boring tasks or high-pressure, produce-results-or-else gigs.

We're talking about work that

- engages us at every level;
- allows us to put our God-given talents and abilities to full use;
- challenges us;
- gives us a vital role in the workings of heaven.

More to the point, we're talking about work done in God's presence. Can you think of someone you really wanted to please, someone whose opinion of your work really mattered to you—whether he or she was a corporate vice president, shift supervisor, parent, or grandparent? Do you remember how good it felt to receive their words of praise for a job well done? Imagine being able to please God with the work you do.

"You are a good and faithful servant. I left you in charge of only a little, but now I will put you in charge of much more. Come and share in my happiness!" (Matthew 25:23). Can you imagine a greater thrill than having those words spoken to you by the Creator of the universe? That opportunity awaits you in heaven.

> "The body of Benjamin Franklin, Printer, lies here, food for worms; but the work shall not be lost, for it will appear once more in a new and more elegant edition, revised and corrected by the Author."
>
> Benjamin Franklin

Read It for Yourself
PROVERBS 12:11

Hard working farmers have more
  than enough food;
daydreamers are nothing more
  than stupid fools.

TRANSFORMERS

Take away sickness. Take away disease. Take away injury and disability. Take away chromosomal disorders. Take away organ damage. Take away the need for artificial limbs. Take away the ravages of time—and the aging process, for that matter.

Take away limits on the ability to reason, discern, and learn. Take away addictions and compulsions. Take away destructive behavior. Take away emotional trauma. Take away every affliction that contains the word *disorder* or *disease*. Take away guilt, shame, regret, and self-loathing.

What are we left with?

Us, in heaven.

Glorious. Strong. Immortal.

In our God-designed, transformed heavenly bodies, we will know a kind of health and wholeness we've never experienced before. In fact, the full implications of having such a transformed body—and mind—may be too complex and overwhelming for our earthly, untransformed minds to comprehend.

Try thinking of it this way. On the best day of your earthly life—the day you felt most healthy, most energetic, most alive—you were operating at a fraction of your God-given potential. In heaven, you will operate at 100 percent capacity. Only in the presence of God will you discover what you are truly capable of. Once you do, however, you'll be able to express and enjoy it for eternity.

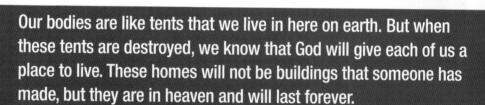

Our bodies are like tents that we live in here on earth. But when these tents are destroyed, we know that God will give each of us a place to live. These homes will not be buildings that someone has made, but they are in heaven and will last forever.

2 Corinthians 5:1

Read It for Yourself
1 CORINTHIANS 15:43, 53

These ugly and weak bodies will become beautiful and strong. . . . Our dead and decaying bodies will be changed into bodies that won't die or decay.

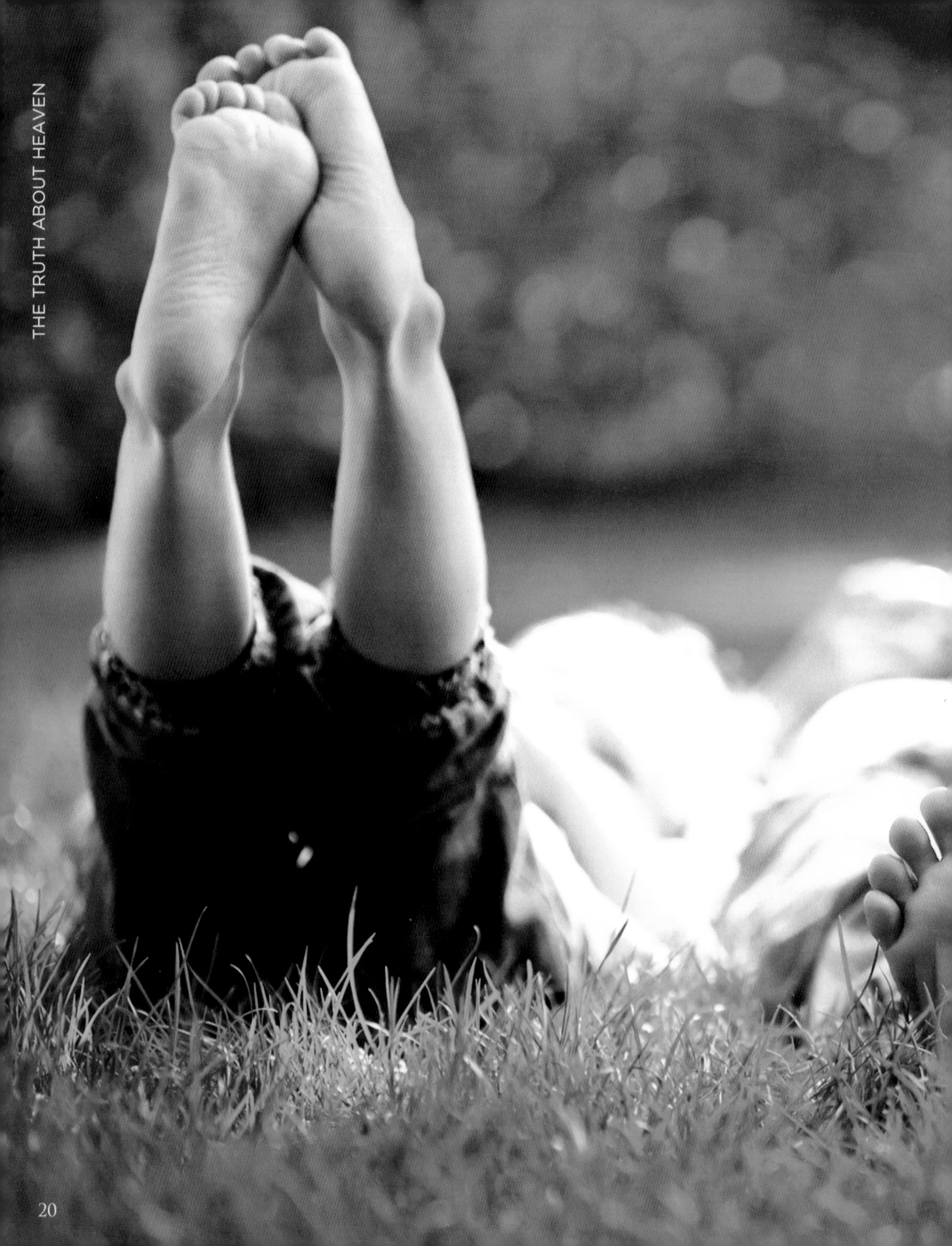

"I am conscious of a soul-sense that lifts me above the narrow, cramping circumstances of my life. My physical limitations are forgotten—my world lies upward, the length and the breadth and the sweep of the heavens are mine!"

— Helen Keller, *The Story of My Life*

TOGETHER AGAIN, FOREVER

For biblical evidence that we will recognize our loved ones in the hereafter, take a look at 2 Samuel 12:23, where David consoles himself after the loss of his newborn son with the knowledge that he "*someday . . . will join him.*" See also the story of the rich man and Lazarus in Luke 16:19–31, in which the rich man recognizes not only Lazarus, whom he knew in life, but also the patriarch Abraham.

Will our earthly memories carry over into eternity? Will we recognize our friends and loved ones in heaven? Though these questions may not be matters of life and death (eternally speaking), they certainly color our outlook on the afterlife. Who among us, after all, hasn't longed to be reunited with a dearly departed loved one—or dreamed of sharing heaven with the people closest to us?

Perhaps a good starting point in addressing these questions of recognition and reunion is to quote George MacDonald, the famed Scottish author and minister, who asked, "Shall we be greater fools in Paradise than we are here?"

His words echo the sentiments of the apostle Paul, who wrote, *"Now all we can see of God is like a cloudy picture in a mirror. Later we will see him face to face. We don't know everything, but then we will, just as God completely understands us"* (1 Corinthians 13:12).

Not only will we know one another in heaven but we will know one another better than we do now. Our faculties will be sharper, thanks to our transformed bodies and minds. That transformation will do wonders for our interpersonal interactions in heaven.

Our relationships will be free from the drama, jealousy, and misunderstandings that plague us in this world. We'll be able to interact with our loved ones (and others) as God intends us to, with nothing to hide: no hidden agendas, no suspect motives, no festering resentments, no damaging competitiveness, no sibling rivalries, no emotional neediness.

Together, as we've never been before, we will enjoy an eternity in God's presence.

Read It for Yourself
LUKE 16:19-31

There was once a rich man who wore expensive clothes and every day ate the best food. But a poor beggar named Lazarus was brought to the gate of the rich man's house. He was happy just to eat the scraps that fell from the rich man's table. His body was covered with sores, and dogs kept coming up to lick them. The poor man died, and angels took him to the place of honor next to Abraham.

The rich man also died and was buried. He went to hell and was suffering terribly. When he looked up and saw Abraham far off and Lazarus at his side, he said to Abraham, "Have pity on me! Send Lazarus to dip his finger in water and touch my tongue. I'm suffering terribly in this fire."

Abraham answered, "My friend, remember that while you lived, you had everything good, and Lazarus had everything bad. Now he is happy, and you are in pain. And besides, there is a deep ditch between us, and no one from either side can cross over."

But the rich man said, "Abraham, then please send Lazarus to my father's home. Let him warn my five brothers, so they won't come to this horrible place."

Abraham answered, "Your brothers can read what Moses and the prophets wrote. They should pay attention to that."

Then the rich man said, "No, that's not enough! If only someone from the dead would go to them, they would listen and turn to God."

So Abraham said, "If they won't pay attention to Moses and the prophets, they won't listen even to someone who comes back from the dead."

AND HEAVEN AND NATURE SING

The psalmists understood that music is a way to God's heart.

Shout praises to the LORD,
  everyone on this earth.
Be joyful and sing
as you come in
  to worship the LORD! (Psalm 100:1–2)

Praise God with trumpets
  and all kinds of harps.
Praise him with tambourines
  and dancing,
with stringed instruments
  and woodwinds.
Praise God with cymbals,
  with clashing cymbals. (Psalm 150:3–5)

So did the apostle Paul: "Let the Spirit fill your life. When you meet together, sing psalms, hymns, and spiritual songs, as you praise the Lord with all your heart" (Ephesians 5:18b–19).

So did Beethoven, for that matter, who once said, "Music is the language of God." It stands to reason, then, that the closer one gets to God's presence, the more music one can expect to hear. Heaven will be filled with music.

Choir members and worship leaders will rejoice (most likely in song) at this prospect. For others, however, scenarios like the one described in Revelation 19 may give pause. The apostle John wrote about "a lot of voices in heaven" shouting together to give praise and worship to the Lord—an inspiring scene,

to be sure, somewhat reminiscent of a grand worship service. And therein lies the pause: the thought of an eternal hymn sing.

What guarantee do we have that we will enjoy the inescapable music (and shouting and noise) of heaven? If by chance we don't like it, won't eternity seem like a very, very long time?

Though the Bible is silent on the topic, there are three factors to consider:

(1) We're talking about the presence of God, the Creator, who is the source of all *creativity*. Something uninspired cannot exist in his presence. What's more, his standards are infinitely higher than ours. So, if something pleases him, it will be awe-inspiring to us.

(2) We will be operating with transformed bodies and minds. Beethoven struggled with hearing loss for a significant portion of his earthly life, and look what he accomplished. Imagine what he might have done had he been endowed with perfect health, perfect clarity of thought, and life eternal. While you're at it, imagine the rest of humanity's greatest musicians *transformed*—able to use every bit of their creativity and skills to compose songs in response to the glorious sights surrounding them in heaven.

(3) There are wild cards in the heavenly deck: angels. God's heavenly messengers have been created with the ability to worship their Creator. Imagine the skills that angels possess. The music they create will likely be nothing like—and exponentially better than—anything we've ever heard.

You have rescued me!
  I will celebrate and shout,
singing praises to you
  with all my heart.
Psalm 71:23

NO-CRY ZONE

The Bible gives us promises of what we can look forward to in heaven:

> *God will wipe all tears from their eyes, and there will be no more death, suffering, crying, or pain. These things of the past are gone forever.* (Revelation 21:4)

> *The people the LORD has rescued*
> *will come back singing*
> *as they enter Zion.*
> *Happiness will be a crown*
> *everyone will always wear.*
> *They will celebrate and shout*
> *because all sorrows and worries*
> *will be gone far away.* (Isaiah 35:10)

On the one hand, these promises of no sadness or mourning in heaven are a welcome relief. Heaven knows we've had enough sorrow, grief, pain, and suffering here on earth to last a lifetime. (Granted, our miseries have largely been of our own making in this fallen world, but that doesn't make them any easier to bear.) Having that day, when all sadness will cease, to look forward to gives us hope.

On the other hand, the absence of sadness and mourning in heaven seems a little cold—unnatural even. After all, it's not likely that every one of our loved ones and acquaintances is a professing Christian. The brutal truth is that all of us know and care about people who, as far as we're aware (and despite our best efforts), are destined for hell.

If that's the case, why isn't sadness mentioned as a predominant emotion in heaven? How can we not mourn, knowing that the people we care about will be separated from God forever? How can sadness be extinguished in the midst of such tragic circumstances?

The Bible offers no definitive answer. The best explanation likely involves the transformation of our bodies and minds: *"But we are citizens of heaven and are eagerly waiting for our Savior to come from there. Our Lord Jesus Christ has power over everything, and he will make these poor bodies of ours like his own glorious body"* (Philippians 3:20–21).

Perhaps sadness and grief, as we experience them, are the results of our partial understanding. Perhaps when we receive new, heavenly bodies, we will view eternity from God's perspective and be able to move beyond our earthly emotions.

He will wipe all tears from their eyes, and there will be no more death, suffering, crying, or pain. These things of the past are gone forever.

Revelation 21:4

SLAVES NO MORE

Sin in heaven? The idea isn't as far-fetched as it may seem. In fact, there's a precedent. Lucifer, created as an angel, enjoyed unfettered access to God's presence. Yet Lucifer's pride caused him to lead a rebellion in heaven against God. In so doing, he brought evil into existence.

Will that evil reach heaven again in eternity? Some Bible scholars declare it an impossibility. They contend that even the potential for sin is nonexistent. And they point to passages such as Hebrews 9:26–28 to support their contention:

> If [Christ] had offered himself every year, he would have suffered many times since the creation of the world. But instead, near the end of time he offered himself once and for all, so he could be a sacrifice that does away with sin.
>
> We die only once, and then we are judged. So Christ died only once to take away the sins of many people. But when he comes again, it will not be to take away sin. He will come to save everyone who is waiting for him.

There's a finality to these words. Jesus died once for all sin, eliminating the possibility of his ever having to do it again. His victory over sin is eternal.

Having said that, the Bible gives no indication that free will is revoked in heaven, a fact that is both understandable and a little worrisome.

It is understandable because praise and worship (two notable heavenly passions) are made meaningful by free will. Would God be able to take genuine pleasure in praise that he himself generated by "compelling" us to worship?

But it is worrisome because of our track record. We chose to reject God and his authority by exercising our free will. What's to keep us from doing the same thing in heaven?

The simple answer is our transformed minds and bodies.

With our renewed minds and bodies comes a renewed perspective and outlook. We will be able to recognize sin for what it is.

Much of our wrongdoing on earth can be attributed to ignorance or a lack of perspective. We choose to do the wrong thing because it seems expedient or attractive. Often we can't see beyond immediate gratification to the long-term harm. We can't fully understand the effects of sin on our

- relationship with God;
- reputation;
- physical health;
- emotional well-being.

That won't be the case in heaven. With our renewed and improved minds, we will understand the full implications of every choice we face. We'll be wise enough to avoid wrong.

Read It for Yourself
GALATIANS 5:1, 13–14

Christ has set us free! This means we are really free. Now hold on to your freedom and don't ever become slaves of the Law again. . . .

My friends, you were chosen to be free. So don't use your freedom as an excuse to do anything you want. Use it as an opportunity to serve each other with love. All the Law says can be summed up in the command to love others as much as you love yourself.

WELL DONE, GOOD AND FAITHFUL SERVANT

When it comes to securing eternal life or atoning for our sins, our good works are worthless. The apostle Paul couldn't be any clearer on that point: *"You were saved by faith in God, who treats us much better than we deserve. This is God's gift to you, and not anything you have done on your own. It isn't something you have earned, so there is nothing you can brag about"* (Ephesians 2:8–9).

With that said, Scripture also makes it clear that we, as believers, are rewarded in heaven for our faithfulness during our time on earth. God sees the work we do on his behalf, the suffering we endure because of our association with him, and the desire we have to live according to his Word. And he acknowledges our deeds in a very real and meaningful way. Jesus himself said so.

> *God will bless you when people insult you, mistreat you, and tell all kinds of evil lies about you because of me. Be happy and excited! You will have a great reward in heaven. People did these same things to the prophets who lived long ago.* (Matthew 5:11–12)
>
> *When you do good deeds, don't try to show off. If you do, you won't get a reward from your Father in heaven.*
>
> *When you give to the poor, don't blow a loud horn. That's what show-offs do in the synagogues and on the street corners, because they are always looking for praise. I can assure you that they already have their reward.*
>
> *When you give to the poor, don't let anyone know about it. Then your gift will be given in secret.*
>
> *Your Father knows what is done in secret and will reward you.*

> *When you pray, don't be like those show-offs who love to stand up and pray in the synagogues and on the street corners. They do this just to look good. I can assure you that they already have their reward.*
>
> *When you pray, go into a room alone and close the door. Pray to your Father in private. He knows what is done in private and will reward you.* (Matthew 6:1–6)

Jesus makes an important distinction between acts that glorify ourselves and acts that glorify God. Only the latter will be rewarded in heaven.

It's noteworthy, especially in today's "everyone-gets-the-same-size-trophy-just-for-participating" culture, that the amount (or degree) of rewards will differ from person to person. *"The Son of Man will soon come in the glory of his Father and with his angels to reward all people for what they have done"* (Matthew 16:27).

Jesus expanded on this principle in the parable of the three servants (Matthew 25:14–20). What it boils down to is this: what you do with what you've been given on earth determines how you're rewarded in heaven. Those who do more with their spiritual gifts, natural abilities, and difference-making opportunities will be more richly rewarded than those who squander them.

The details of heaven's reward system aren't spelled out in Scripture. Suffice it to say, God keeps track of the work that is done in his name and richly rewards his workers.

PURGATORY: HEAVEN PREP

Read It for Yourself

1 CORINTHIANS 3:14–15

We will be rewarded if our building is left standing. But if it is destroyed by the fire, we will lose everything. Yet we ourselves will be saved, like someone escaping from flames.

When believers die, do their souls go directly to heaven? Or is there a destination between here and there—a place where souls are made ready for God's presence? Most Protestant Christians lean toward the direct-route view of heaven. Many Catholic Christians, on the other hand, believe in an intermediate state called purgatory.

Purgatory, as it is explained in the catechism of the Catholic Church, features elements of heaven and hell. Only the souls of those "who die in God's grace and friendship" enter purgatory. Yet the process of purification—of making souls ready for heaven—may involve anything from an extreme awareness of loss to an intensely painful fire (though not the kind of painful fire experienced by people who are condemned to hell).

The souls of the people remain in purgatory until all the sins they failed to deal with on earth are cleansed. In some cases, that process may take a few hours. In others, it may take a few million years, depending on the severity of the sins in question.

In addition to the soul's experiences in purgatory, purification may be aided by the intercession of Catholics who are still living. Intercession can involve saying the Mass, praying the Rosary, and performing acts of penance.

Protestant Christians—a group that includes members of the Anglican, Baptist, Lutheran, Methodist, and Presbyterian denominations (to name a few)—who object to the doctrine of purgatory point out that

- its tenets are not spelled out in Scripture but instead come from the Apocrypha and the writings of the church fathers;
- the necessity of further purification after we die suggests that Jesus' sacrifice is insufficient to cleanse our sins;
- it contradicts the apostle Paul's assertion that justification comes through faith alone;
- it places too much power and responsibility in the hands of human beings for effecting the purification of souls.

HELL: AN ETERNAL SEPARATION?

If heaven is the eternal experience of God's presence, then hell must be the eternal experience of separation from him, right?

Yes and no.

The Bible certainly speaks in those terms.

> Our Lord Jesus will punish anyone who doesn't know God and won't obey his message. Their punishment will be eternal destruction, and they will be kept far from the presence of our Lord and his glorious strength. (2 Thessalonians 1:8b–9)

> On the day of judgment many will call me their Lord. They will say, "We preached in your name, and in your name we forced out demons and worked many miracles." But I will tell them, "I will have nothing to do with you! Get out of my sight, you evil people!" (Matthew 7:22–23)

Yet is it a separation, per se? God, after all, is omnipresent. He is everywhere at once. No place is beyond his reach or off-limits to his presence. The psalmist expresses that fact in no uncertain terms.

> Where could I go to escape
> from your Spirit
>   or from your sight?
> If I were to climb up
> to the highest heavens,
>   you would be there.
> If I were to dig down
> to the world of the dead
>   you would also be there.
> Suppose I had wings
> like the dawning day
>   and flew across the ocean.
> Even then your powerful arm
>   would guide and protect me.
>   (Psalm 139:7–10)

Perhaps a better way to describe the spiritual reality of hell is found in the Westminster Larger Catechism (Question 29): "an everlasting separation from the comfortable presence of God." The souls in hell will experience God's holiness and wrath, but none of his grace or mercy.

Whereas God's presence in heaven will be a source of joy and celebration, in hell the separation from his presence will cause torment. Hell is a separation from all that is good and comforting about God's presence.

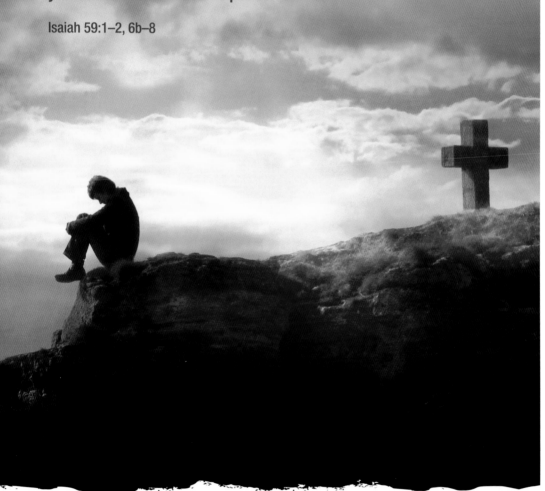

The LORD hasn't lost his powerful strength; he can still hear and answer prayers. Your sins are the roadblock between you and your God. That's why he doesn't answer your prayers or let you see his face. . . . You're sinful and brutal. You hurry off to do wrong or murder innocent victims. All you think about is sin; you leave ruin and destruction wherever you go. You don't know how to live in peace or to be fair with others. The roads you make are crooked; your followers cannot find peace.

Isaiah 59:1–2, 6b–8

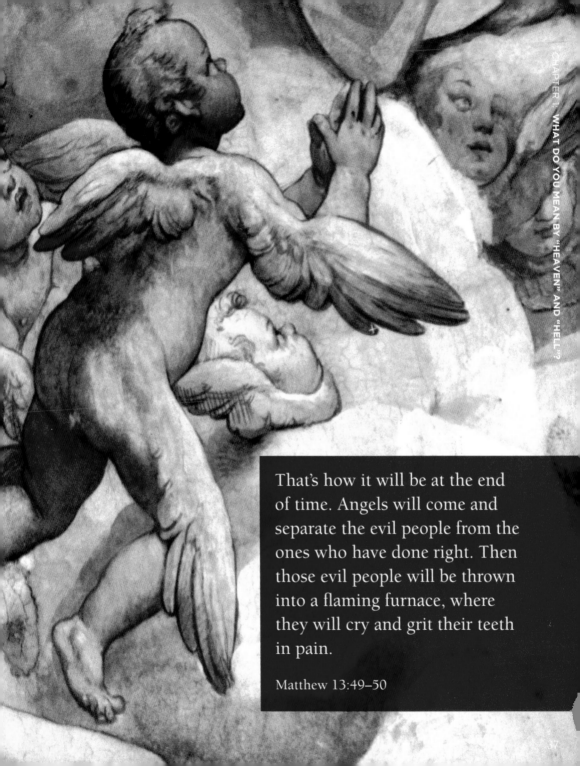

That's how it will be at the end of time. Angels will come and separate the evil people from the ones who have done right. Then those evil people will be thrown into a flaming furnace, where they will cry and grit their teeth in pain.

Matthew 13:49–50

THE REALITY OF HELL

CHAPTER 1: WHAT DO YOU MEAN BY "HEAVEN" AND "HELL"?

How can one place be a lake of fire (Revelation 20:14) and a deep pit (Revelation 20:1–3)? How can that same place be filled with inextinguishable flames (Mark 9:43) and darkness (Matthew 8:12) at the same time?

One obvious response: *This is God we're talking about. The laws of physics don't apply to him. He can do anything he wants.*

And who could argue with such theology?

But if the Bible writers—and Jesus himself— were referring to a flame that adheres to none of the physical properties of fire as we understand it, why would they use the word *fire?*

Perhaps our wisest approach to the topic of hell is to acknowledge, as most Bible scholars do, that there is some degree of symbolism in the Bible's descriptions. The question is, which parts should be interpreted literally and which should be interpreted symbolically? The place to start is with hell itself.

Is hell an actual place or a symbolic description of a spiritual state?

Jesus used an actual place as a point of reference when he talked about hell. The word translated as "hell" in Mark 9:43–48 is "Gehenna." Gehenna was considered an abominable place by Jesus' Jewish audience. Centuries earlier, their ancestors had sacrificed their children to the god Molech in the valley where Gehenna was located. In Jesus' day, the site was a garbage dump

outside Jerusalem—a worm-infested place where a fire burned incessantly.

The apostle John's description of the final judgment also refers to hell in physical terms.

> Then the devil who fooled them will be thrown into the lake of fire and burning sulfur. He will be there with the beast and the false prophet, and they will be in pain day and night forever and ever. (Revelation 20:10)

> But I will tell you what will happen to cowards and to everyone who is unfaithful or dirty-minded or who murders or is sexually immoral or uses witchcraft or worships idols or tells lies. They will be thrown into that lake of fire and burning sulfur. This is the second death. (Revelation 21:8)

Based on these passages and others, many Bible scholars and Christian denominations hold to the belief that hell is a location—a place where those who reject God's gift of salvation and eternal life will endure the consequences of their decision.

HELLFIRE AND DAMNATION

The fires of hell are the pop-culture equivalent of clouds and harps in heaven. They top the list of clichés involving afterlife destinations. Cartoons are the primary purveyors of the clichés. If an animator needs to represent hell, you can bet fire will be involved. Tom and Jerry, Daffy Duck, Yosemite Sam, and Homer Simpson all have been singed by hell's flames to varying degrees of comic effect.

Strange that such an agonizing aspect of Christian theology would be appropriated for broad comedy.

The Bible certainly allows no room for humor in its descriptions of hell's flames.

> [Jesus'] threshing fork is in his hand, and he is ready to separate the wheat from the husks. He will store the wheat in a barn and burn the husks in a fire that never goes out. (Matthew 3:12)

> You will have to drink the wine that God gives to everyone who makes him angry. You will feel his mighty anger, and you will be tortured with fire and burning sulfur, while the holy angels and the Lamb look on. (Revelation 14:10)

If these descriptions are meant to be taken literally, we may conclude that hellfire is unlike any flame known to modern science. Apparently, it causes excruciating pain, yet it does not consume that which it burns. (In that sense, it is different from the fire of judgment God rained on Sodom and Gomorrah.) The Bible gives no indication as to what fuels hell's flames.

If the descriptions are meant to be taken figuratively, it probably won't make much of a difference to those who are condemned to hell. The agony described in Scripture is very real, whether it is caused by fire or by some less readily identifiable source.

Read It for Yourself
MATTHEW 25:41-46

Then the king will say to those on his left, "Get away from me! You are under God's curse. Go into the everlasting fire prepared for the devil and his angels! I was hungry, but you did not give me anything to eat, and I was thirsty, but you did not give me anything to drink. I was a stranger, but you did not welcome me, and I was naked, but you did not give me any clothes to wear. I was sick and in jail, but you did not take care of me."

Then the people will ask, "Lord, when did we fail to help you when you were hungry or thirsty or a stranger or naked or sick or in jail?"

The king will say to them, "Whenever you failed to help any of my people, no matter how unimportant they seemed, you failed to do it for me."

Then Jesus said, "Those people will be punished forever. But the ones who pleased God will have eternal life."

Descent into Hell (detail), c. 1468
Dieric Bouts (c. 1415–1475)

DARK AS A DUNGEON

Read It for Yourself
2 THESSALONIANS 1:8b–10a

Our Lord Jesus will punish anyone who doesn't know God and won't obey his message. Their punishment will be eternal destruction, and they will be kept far from the presence of our Lord and his glorious strength. This will happen on that day when the Lord returns to be praised and honored by all who have faith in him and belong to him.

I n certain music genres, hell has become something of a cliché—a go-to device for songwriters looking to suggest, of all things, a good time. Call it the "I'd-Rather-Party-Forever-with-the-Damned-Than-Worship-Forever-with-the-Redeemed Syndrome."

This line of thinking recasts hell as some kind of mid-August Texas barbeque. Sweltering? Yes. But bearable—especially if it's a dry heat. And it's made more bearable by the fact that all of one's rowdy friends will be there too. In short, when viewed as a communal experience, hell doesn't seem so bad.

The Bible, however, gives no indication that hell will be a communal experience. In fact, in his parable of the three servants, Jesus suggested that hell may be more solitary than we imagine. *"You are a worthless servant, and you will be thrown out into the dark where people will cry and grit their teeth in pain"* (Matthew 25:30).

Jesus wasn't referring to just any darkness; this kind of outer darkness is far removed from everyone and everything. Such an extreme and desolate darkness pervading hell should not surprise us.

Jesus told us God is light and doesn't have any darkness in him. Now we are telling you. (1 John 1:5)

And the city did not need the sun or the moon. The glory of God was shining on it, and the Lamb was its light. (Revelation 21:23)

God is the source of light. In the absence of his presence, darkness will reign.

In speaking of darkness, the Bible suggests something more torturous than simply a permanent night. The darkness of hell will be oppressive and figure prominently in people's suffering. To make matters worse, the darkness of hell will be isolating. There will be no reunions of rowdy friends, no group dynamics, no shared experiences.

The darkness of hell will likely ensure that those condemned to its blackness will serve their eternal sentence in solitary confinement.

A Vision of Hell from Dante's *Divine Comedy*
Illustration by Gustave Doré (1832–1883)

A SEPARATE AGONY

Pop culture has given us no shortage of scenarios as to how people might be made to suffer in hell. One popular theme is ironic punishment. The inveterate gambler wins every bet he makes, thus the thrill is ruined. The doughnut lover is force-fed crullers and Boston cream–filled fried cakes—ad infinitum.

In reality, though, the very nature of hell—the absence of God's presence—may be its most excruciating feature. To understand, we need to look back to Jesus' crucifixion.

In order to be a perfect sacrifice for us, Jesus *became* sin on the cross, which put him at odds with God's holiness. So when Jesus became sin, God removed his presence from his Son. In a sense, Jesus experienced hell during that time on the cross.

Already he had been savagely beaten by soldiers. His beard had been pulled out. He had spikes driven through his wrists and feet. He was lifted up on a rough wooden cross, held in place only by his impaled body parts. He had a crown of thorns shoved into his head. He had been abandoned by his closest friends and mocked by his enemies.

Through it all, Jesus displayed astonishing serenity. He prayed for the people who tortured and mocked him. He maintained a dignified silence in the face of unimaginable indignities.

One agony, though, overwhelmed him: *"Then about that time Jesus shouted, 'Eli, Eli, lema sabachthani?' which means, 'My God, my God, why have you deserted me?' "* (Matthew 27:46).

The removal of God's presence was incalculably more excruciating to Jesus than any physical or emotional torture. And if that removal affected Jesus in such an extreme manner, imagine what it will do to the people in hell.

> The story of the rich man and Lazarus in Luke 16:19–31 suggests that thirst will also factor into people's suffering in hell.

GOD WILL REWARD EACH OF US FOR WHAT WE HAVE DONE. HE WILL GIVE ETERNAL LIFE TO EVERYONE WHO HAS PATIENTLY DONE WHAT IS GOOD IN THE HOPE OF RECEIVING GLORY, HONOR, AND LIFE THAT LASTS FOREVER. BUT HE WILL SHOW HOW ANGRY AND FURIOUS HE CAN BE WITH EVERY SELFISH PERSON WHO REJECTS THE TRUTH AND WANTS TO DO EVIL.

ROMANS 2:6–8

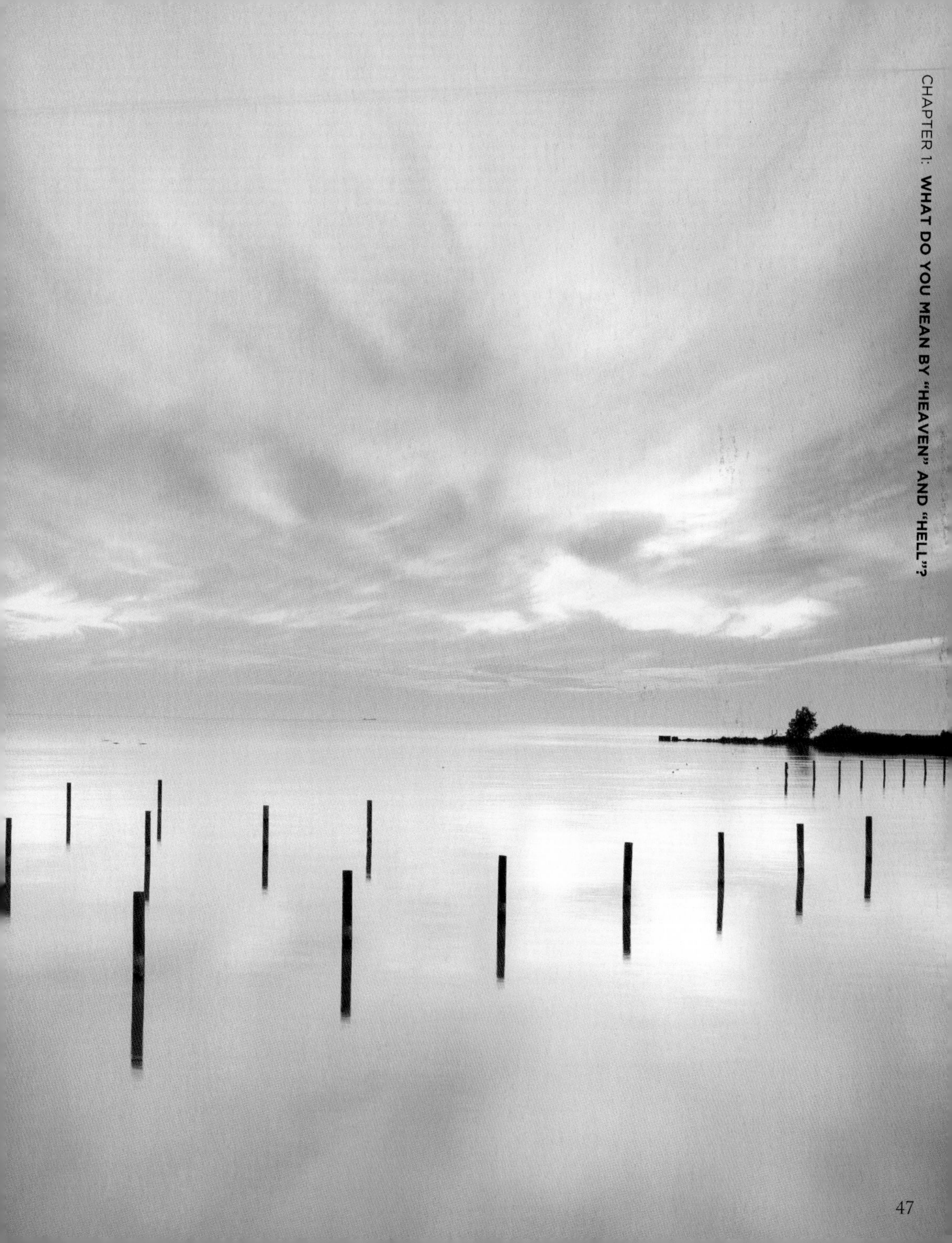

The Damned, c. 1620, Peter Paul Rubens (1577–1640)

REGRETS ONLY

Revelation 21:3–4 describes the eternal state of well-being we will experience in heaven: *"God's home is now with his people. He will live with them, and they will be his own. Yes, God will make his home among his people. He will wipe all tears from their eyes, and there will be no more death, suffering, crying, or pain. These things of the past are gone forever."*

In stark contrast to heaven's scene of emotional healing is the painful reality of hell: *"Then [the Son of Man] will throw them into a flaming furnace, where people will cry and grit their teeth in pain"* (Matthew 13:42).

Jesus offers no comfort, no resolution, and no prospect of relief for those who will suffer the emotional trauma of hell.

In darkness and solitude, they will be overwhelmed with regret. They will spend eternity with their thoughts and memories. They will recall every exposure they had to the truth about Jesus. They will relive every time they rejected God's gift of salvation. They will kick themselves over and over again for their hard-heartedness and their skewed earthly priorities. They will wrestle forevermore with the question "What if?"

The pangs of regret, as well as the realization that they will not be given a second chance, will leave them in constant agony. They will know what it is like to be separated from God, with no hope of reconciliation.

Jesus' story of the rich man and Lazarus in Luke 16 raises one more specter that will haunt the people of hell: the fate of their unbelieving loved ones. The rich man in hell begs Abraham to send Lazarus back to earth to warn his brothers about the fate that awaits them. You'll notice that the man's memories of earth are vivid—and emotionally painful.

Abraham points out that not even a visit from the great beyond could persuade someone who is committed to unbelief. The rich man—like everyone in hell—is left to curse his earthly choices, his indifference (until it was too late), and his failure to be a better example to his loved ones.

Read It for Yourself
REVELATION 20:11–15

I saw a great white throne with someone sitting on it. Earth and heaven tried to run away, but there was no place for them to go. I also saw all the dead people standing in front of that throne. Every one of them was there, no matter who they had once been. Several books were opened, and then the book of life was opened. The dead were judged by what those books said they had done.

The sea gave up the dead people who were in it, and death and its kingdom also gave up their dead. Then everyone was judged by what they had done. Afterwards, death and its kingdom were thrown into the lake of fire. This is the second death. Anyone whose name wasn't written in the book of life was thrown into the lake of fire.

JUST DESERTS

A*t least I'm not as bad as . . ."*

How many times have those words been used to try to justify wrong behavior?

In Dante's Inferno, the nine circles of hell are built on the premise that not all sins are equally heinous or sinners equally punished. Dante's first circle (which is actually closer to an imperfect version of heaven) is reserved for virtuous non-Christians. From there, the sins grow progressively worse, from lust to anger to treachery (treachery being the ninth circle). The corresponding punishments in each circle become progressively more severe as well.

Perhaps the coldest comfort of all is that Dante's premise has eternal validity. Bible passages such as Revelation 20:12–13 suggest that people will face varying degrees of punishment in hell, based on their actions during their lifetimes.

Just as God rewards believers for their earthly work on his behalf, so he will make unbelievers pay for their egregious offenses against him and others. The Bible offers no official "pecking order" of sins, as Dante did. It does, however, reveal some surprising truths about who will receive an extra measure of punishment.

Look at Jesus' words in Matthew 11:21–22:

You people of Chorazin are in for trouble! You people of Bethsaida are in for trouble too! If the miracles that took place here had happened in Tyre and Sidon, the people there would have turned to God long ago. They would have dressed in sackcloth and put ashes on their heads. I tell you on the day of judgment the people of Tyre and Sidon will get off easier than you will.

Chorazin and Bethsaida were Jewish cities where Jesus had preached extensively and performed countless miracles. Despite all they had heard and seen, the people of these cities continued to reject him, making themselves more deserving of a harsher punishment than the Gentile peoples of Tyre and Sidon. Though the people of Tyre and Sidon were notorious for wickedness, their lack of exposure to Jesus and his message made them less deserving of punishment, as far as God was concerned.

We may conclude, then, that people bound for hell are judged and punished according to how extensively they were exposed to the truth about Christ, and how many times they rejected it.

> "Through me you go into a city of weeping; through me you go into eternal pain; through me you go amongst the lost people."
>
> Dante, *The Inferno*

Read It for Yourself
ROMANS 2:1–4

Some of you accuse others of doing wrong. But there is no excuse for what you do. When you judge others, you condemn yourselves, because you are guilty of doing the very same things. We know that God is right to judge everyone who behaves in this way. Do you really think God won't punish you, when you behave exactly like the people you accuse? You surely don't think much of God's wonderful goodness or of his patience and willingness to put up with you. Don't you know that the reason God is good to you is because he wants you to turn to him?

above: *The Panderers, Seducers, and Flatterers,* Eighth Circle of Dante's Inferno, c.15th century, Sandro Botticelli (1445–1510)

MANY OF THOSE WHO LIE
DEAD IN THE GROUND
WILL RISE FROM DEATH.
SOME OF THEM WILL BE
GIVEN ETERNAL LIFE, AND
OTHERS WILL RECEIVE
NOTHING BUT ETERNAL
SHAME AND DISGRACE.
EVERYONE WHO HAS
BEEN WISE WILL SHINE AS
BRIGHT AS THE SKY ABOVE,
AND EVERYONE WHO HAS
LED OTHERS TO PLEASE
GOD WILL SHINE FOREVER
LIKE THE STARS.

DANIEL 12:2–3

THE PROBLEM WITH HAPPILY EVER AFTER

The idea of an afterlife apart from God is hard enough to come to grips with. Throw in the specter of eternal *suffering*—in fire and darkness, no less—and you have a theological concept that flies in the face of the basic human desire for "happily ever after."

Perhaps, then, it is no surprise that the concept of universalism has achieved a certain measure of acceptance in our society. Universalism is the belief that all human beings will be saved eventually.

Universalists are eternal optimists with utopian sentiments. But when it comes to understanding God's plan for the hereafter, we must be able to recognize the fine line between wishful thinking and antibiblical beliefs.

The concept of universalism contradicts dozens of Scriptural principles, including the following:

Universalism renders God's nature imperfect.

Justice and holiness are every bit as inextricable from God's nature as his love and mercy are. If God were to allow everyone into heaven, it would cause him to violate his own justice and holiness, making himself less than perfect.

Universalism makes a liar of Jesus.

The quote is out there for everyone to see. *"I am the way, the truth, and the life! . . . Without me, no one can go to the Father"* (John 14:6). Jesus made it abundantly clear to his followers that no one can receive eternal life without first believing in him. Universalism, in contrast, makes Jesus incidental to salvation. Anyone can believe in anything and still receive eternal life.

Universalism makes Jesus' sacrifice unnecessary.

If God had planned all the while to open the doors of heaven to everyone, then Jesus' death on the cross and resurrection were unnecessary. His sacrifice achieved nothing. It can be ignored and dismissed with no real consequence to our eternal standing.

The doctrine of eternal punishment is agonizing and arguably the most difficult concept Christians must wrestle with. Yet, wrestle we must. To propose any alternative, especially one that contradicts Scripture, is to misrepresent God and give dangerously false hope.

Read It for Yourself
HEBREWS 9:25-27

Christ did not have to offer himself many times. He wasn't like a high priest who goes into the most holy place each year to offer the blood of an animal. If he had offered himself every year, he would have suffered many times since the creation of the world. But instead, near the end of time he offered himself once and for all, so that he could be a sacrifice that does away with sin.

We die only once, and then we are judged. So Christ died only once to take away the sins of many people. But when he comes again, it will not be to take away sin. He will come to save everyone who is waiting for him.

Can God be considered a fair Judge if he imposes a sentence of *eternal* punishment for a *finite* offense? If people commit earthly sins—even one as unforgivable as rejecting God's gift of salvation for a lifetime—should they be made to pay *forever*? Those questions lie at the heart of annihilationism.

Annihilationists believe that God will ultimately destroy, or put out of existence, those who reject him. Some annihilationists believe the destruction occurs at death; others believe it occurs sometime in the afterlife, after a designated period of punishment in hell. They believe that hell is a temporary phenomenon, one that will be done away with after it has served its purpose.

Christians who oppose the concept of annihilationism use Jesus' words in Matthew 25:46 to support their position: *"Those people will be punished forever. But the ones who pleased God will have eternal life."* The Greek word translated "forever" or "eternal" in this passage is used to refer to the destiny of those bound for heaven and those bound for hell. So, if eternal punishment is temporary, then eternal life must also be temporary.

Opponents to annihilationism also point to the apostle John's words in Revelation 20:10: *"Then the devil who fooled them will be thrown into the lake of fire and burning sulfur. He will be there with the beast and the false prophet, and they will be in pain day and night forever and ever."* Those last six words, *"day and night forever and ever,"* leave little wiggle room for suggesting anything other than eternal punishment.

The fact that annihilationism seems to cast God in a more favorable light, or seems to make his justice more palatable to our modern sensibilities, is not a reason to believe in it. As Christians, we're not called to be God's public relations team. We're called to study his Word and build our belief system on what we find there, regardless of how "palatable" it is.

AN END TO THE MISERY?

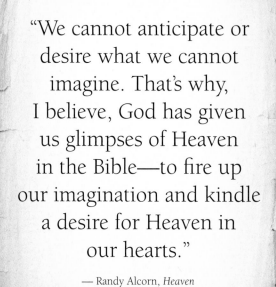

"We cannot anticipate or desire what we cannot imagine. That's why, I believe, God has given us glimpses of Heaven in the Bible—to fire up our imagination and kindle a desire for Heaven in our hearts."

— Randy Alcorn, *Heaven*

CHAPTER 1: **WHAT DO YOU MEAN BY "HEAVEN" AND "HELL"?**

When someone invites you to a party, one of the first questions you ask is, "Who else is going to be there?" It's a perfectly reasonable question. Before you commit to attending, you want to know who you'll be mingling with.

However, when the shindig in question is eternal, knowing who will be there becomes much more relevant.

There is no shortage of opinions as to who deserves to be in heaven or hell, who is already there and who is not. How many times have you heard someone say, "I know my grandma is in heaven right now, watching over us," or "There is a special place in hell for people who abuse children"? While these sentiments are understandable, we must ultimately defer to God's Word on the matter.

Bible passages such as Revelation 3:5 and Philippians 4:3 suggest that God has a list—a book containing the names of everyone who will go to heaven. Though we're not privy to the contents of this book of life, Scripture can help us discern who resides in heaven—and who faces hell.

CHAPTER 2

WHO WILL BE THERE?

For example, we may conclude that the "heavenly who's who" includes the following:

- God—the One whose presence actually creates heaven
- Jesus—the One whose sacrifice makes heaven possible for the human race
- Angels—God's heavenly task force
- The four living creatures and twenty-four elders of Revelation—the mysterious beings that figure prominently in the apostle John's vision of heaven
- Believers—people who trust in Jesus for eternal life

Likewise, we may conclude that "hell dwellers" include the following:

- Satan—the adversary of God and champion of evil
- Demons—the insurgent angels who rebelled against God in heaven and oppose his work on earth
- The antichrist and his minions—the enemies of Christ who are singled out in Revelation for their treachery and deception
- Unbelievers—people who reject God's gift of eternal life

In this section, we'll take a look at these individuals (or groups of individuals) to see what the Bible says about their presence in heaven or hell and what it means to us.

Mural painting from Sucevit Monastery located in Bukovina (northern Romania)

GOD'S IN HIS HEAVEN
ALL'S RIGHT WITH THE WORLD

Choosing mere words to express deep theological concepts can be a tricky exercise, especially when those concepts have to do with God's nature.

Case in point: It's accurate to say, God is in heaven. The Bible makes that clear. The psalmist wrote, *"The LORD looks at the world from his throne in heaven, and he watches us all"* (Psalm 33:13–14).

Jesus—who knew a thing or two about heaven—warned his disciples, *"Don't be cruel to any of these little ones! I promise you their angels are always with my Father in heaven"* (Matthew 18:10–11).

And when he taught his disciples to pray, Jesus addressed his prayer, *"Our Father in heaven . . ."* (Matthew 6:9).

However, theologically speaking, it's inaccurate to say that God *lives* in heaven. The God of Scripture is eternal, ever present, and limitless. He doesn't *live* anywhere—at least, not as we understand dwelling places. But he does choose a place to make his presence known. That place is heaven. So we *can* say that heaven is the inevitable result of God's presence.

Or more succinctly, we can say, *Where God is, there is heaven.*

The New Testament goes so far as to use *heaven* interchangeably with *Yahweh*, the Hebrew name for God. In his parable of the prodigal son, Jesus quoted the repentant young man as saying, *"Father, I have sinned against God in heaven and against you"* (Luke 15:21).

Whatever else heaven may be, it is first and foremost an experience of God's presence. And that's what makes our future so exciting.

James 1:17 says, *"Every good and perfect gift comes down from the Father who created all the lights in the heavens. He is always the same and never makes dark shadows by changing."*

God is the source of everything that is

- ultimately good;
- ultimately fulfilling;
- ultimately pleasing;
- ultimately secure.

It stands to reason that the closer we get to God, the purer and more intense our experiences of goodness, fulfillment, pleasure, and security become.

God the Father Giving His Blessing, Domenico Alfani (c.1479–1553)
Alinari / Art Resource, NY

The Lord looks at the world from his
throne in heaven, and he watches us all.

Psalm 33:13–14

"I do not think that it is wrong for us to think and talk about heaven. I like to locate heaven and find out all I can about it. I expect to live there through all eternity. If I were going to dwell in any place in this country, if I were going to make it my home, I would want to inquire about the place, about its climate, about the neighbors I would have, about everything, in fact, that I could learn concerning it."

— Dwight L. Moody, *Heaven*

JESUS
AT THE RIGHT HAND OF THE FATHER

Christ Giving the Blessings, c. 1492, Fernando Gallego (1440–1507)

If you follow news reports about heroic rescues, or selfless courage in the face of danger, you know the key to a heart-tugging story is the eventual reunion of the rescuers and the would-be victims, who have a chance to say thank-you and pay tribute to their saviors.

With that in mind, take a look at the description of heaven found in Revelation 5:11–13:

As I looked, I heard the voices of a large number of angels around the throne and the voices of the living creatures and of the elders. There were millions and millions of them, and they were saying in a loud voice,

"The Lamb who was killed is worthy to receive power, riches, wisdom, strength, honor, glory, and praise."

Then I heard all beings in heaven and on the earth and under the earth and in the sea offer praise. Together, all of them were saying,

"Praise, honor, glory, and strength forever and ever to the one who sits on the throne and to the Lamb!"

This is the scene of a savior—*the* Savior—receiving the glory and honor due him for his sacrificial "rescue" of the human race.

In 1 Peter 3:18, the apostle Peter emphasized that eternal life in heaven would not be possible without Jesus' death on the cross. Someone had to take the punishment for sin. And only a sinless man could do it.

That is, only Jesus.

He bridged the otherwise unbridgeable gap between God, who is perfect, and humans, who are not.

Heaven gives us the opportunity to show our eternal gratitude for his sacrifice.

"Worthy is the Lamb to receive honor" is a constant refrain heard in the heavenly realm. Jesus is worthy to receive honor because he makes it possible for us to enter God's presence when we die.

It follows, then, that Jesus occupies a place of honor in heaven. Mark 16:19 says Jesus is seated *"at the right side of God."* And from that exalted position, he will reign forever.

Read It for Yourself
HEBREWS 1:1-4

Long ago in many ways and at many times God's prophets spoke his message to our ancestors. But now at last, God sent his Son to bring his message to us. God created the universe by his Son, and everything will someday belong to the Son. God's Son has all the brightness of God's own glory and is like him in every way. By his own mighty word, he holds the universe together.

After the Son had washed away our sins, he sat down at the right side of the glorious God in heaven. He had become much greater than the angels, and the name he was given is far greater than any of theirs.

ANGELS
GOD'S HEAVENLY TASK FORCE

If angels could share one message with the human race, it would undoubtedly involve praising God and bringing glory to him—because that's what angels do.

If angels could share *two* messages with the human race, the second one might go like this: "You will not become one of us after you die. We are uniquely created beings, just as you are. In heaven, we remain angels, and you remain humans.

"P.S. We don't float on clouds, either."

Angels comprise heaven's highly skilled workforce. God created them and gave them specific skills to carry out certain tasks. Occasionally, those tasks involve earthly visits. For example, the angel Gabriel appeared to Mary to tell her that she had been chosen to give birth to the Son of God (Luke 1:26–38). And on the night of Jesus' birth, an unidentified angel appeared to a group of shepherds to announce the arrival of the Savior (Luke 2:8–20). To underscore the importance of the event, *"Suddenly many other angels came down from heaven and joined in praising God"* (Luke 2:13).

The supernatural appearance of angels occasionally causes people to mistake them for deities. In the midst of his apocalyptic vision, the apostle John fell at the feet of an angel to worship him (Revelation 19:9–10). John was quickly corrected by the angel and instructed to worship no one but God. Perhaps that's why the author of Hebrews makes it a point to emphasize that angels are only servants (Hebrews 1:14).

Earthly visits aside, the *raison d'être* of angels is to worship and bring glory to God. You can't swing a stick in the book of Revelation without hitting a passage in which angels are falling prostrate before God's throne or proclaiming his holiness in song. Revelation 4 offers a particularly vivid example of angels in their comfort zone.

Angels are an integral part of the heavenly community. Their praise and worship form the sound track of eternal life. Referring to heaven, the author of Hebrews wrote, *"You have now come to Mount Zion and to the heavenly Jerusalem. This is the city of the living God, where thousands and thousands of angels have come to celebrate"* (12:22).

"The angels glorify; men scrutinize: angels raise their voices in praise; men in disputation: they conceal their faces with their wings; but man with a presumptuous gaze would look into Thine unspeakable Glory."

John Chrysostom

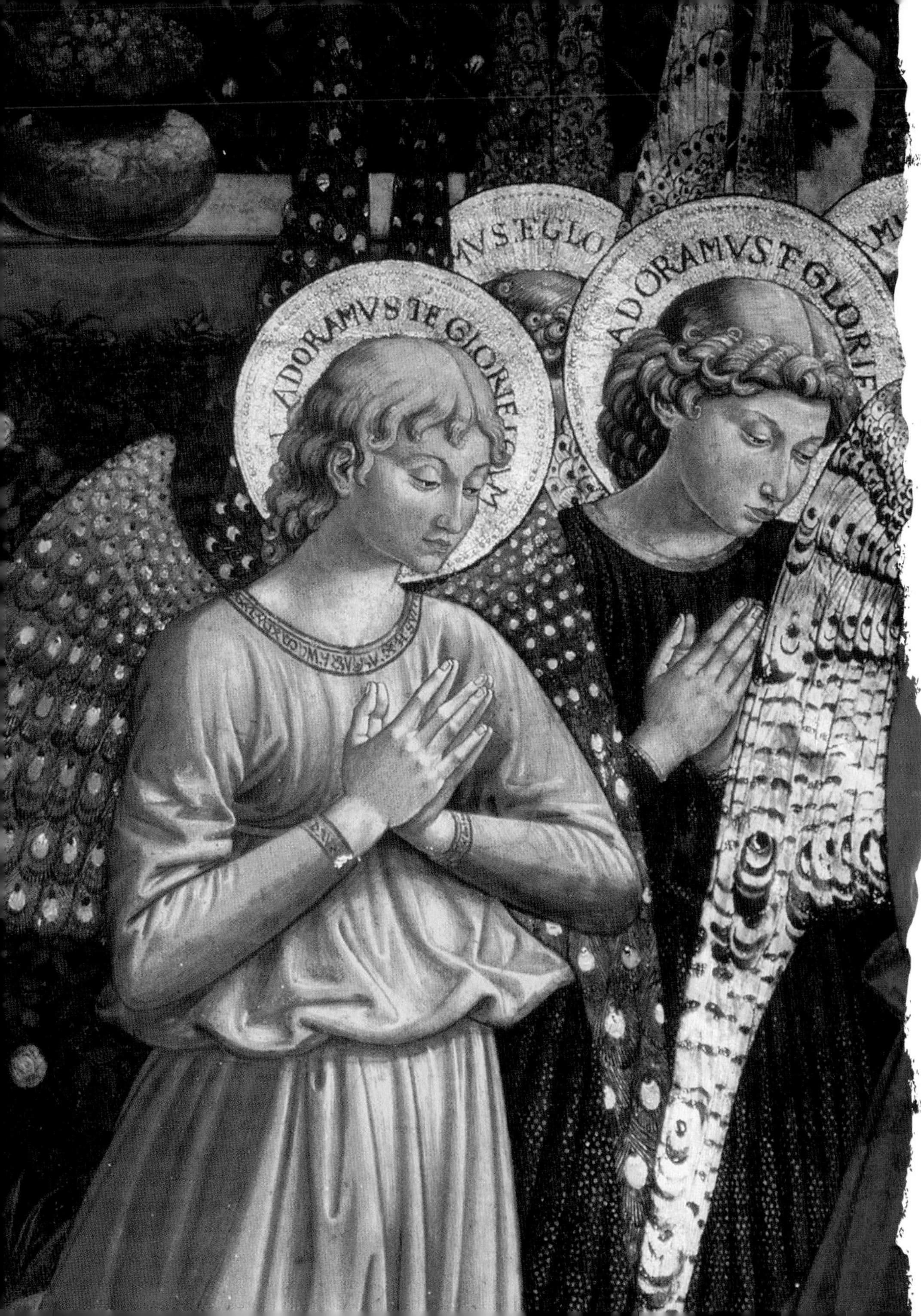
ADORAMVS TE GLORIF

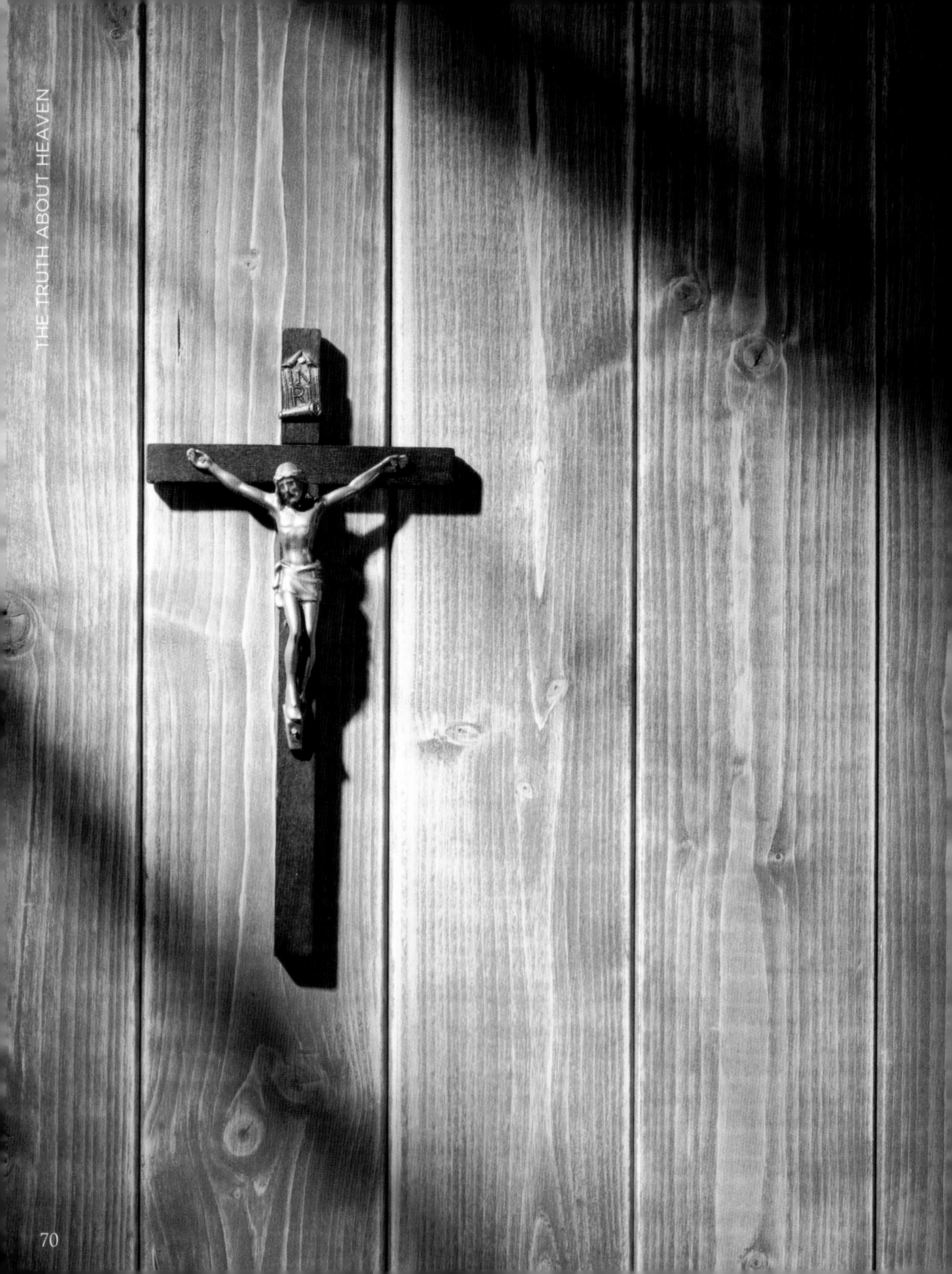
INRI

"It was, to be sure, hell-deserving sinners whom Jesus came to save. All who put their trust in him may know themselves forgiven, justified, and accepted forever—and thus delivered from the wrath to come."

— J. I. Packer

Read It for Yourself
LUKE 1:26–38

One month later God sent the angel Gabriel to the town of Nazareth in Galilee with a message for a virgin named Mary. She was engaged to Joseph from the family of King David. The angel greeted Mary and said, "You are truly blessed! The Lord is with you."

Mary was confused by the angel's words and wondered what they meant. Then the angel told Mary, "Don't be afraid! God is pleased with you, and you will have a son. His name will be Jesus. He will be great and will be called the Son of God Most High. The Lord God will make him king, as his ancestor David was. He will rule the people of Israel forever, and his kingdom will never end."

Mary asked the angel, "How can this happen? I am not even married!"

The angel answered, "The Holy Spirit will come down to you, and God's power will come over you. So your child will be called the holy Son of God. Your relative Elizabeth is also going to have a son, even though she is old. No one thought she could ever have a baby, but in three months she will have a son. Nothing is impossible for God!"

Mary said, "I am the Lord's servant! Let it happen as you have said." And the angel left her.

Mosaic of *The Annunciation* from Santa Maria in Trastevere, Rome, Pietro Cavallini (1250–1330)

MYSTERIOUS CREATURES

SURROUNDING THE THRONE OF HEAVEN

To stand out in the book of Revelation you have to be odd—with a capital *O*. (It is, after all, a book that features locusts with the face of a human, the teeth of a lion, and the sting of a scorpion.) Yet the creatures featured in Revelation 4 manage to do just that—stand out, that is.

The setting is God's heavenly throne. The description is courtesy of the apostle John in his eyewitness account of heaven:

Also in front of the throne was something that looked like a glass sea, clear as crystal.

Around the throne in the center were four living creatures covered front and back with eyes. The first creature was like a lion, the second one was like a bull, the third one had the face of a human, and the fourth was like a flying eagle. Each of the four living creatures had six wings, and their bodies were covered with eyes. Day and night they never stopped singing,

> *"Holy, holy, holy is the Lord,*
> *the all-powerful God,*
> *who was and is*
> *and is coming!"* (Revelation 4:6–8)

Whether this was exactly what John saw, or simply his best attempt to describe the indescribable, is open to debate. What we do know is that these beings play key roles in heaven.

Mentioned in conjunction with these four creatures are the considerably less conspicuous twenty-four elders. These elders are clothed in white and wear gold crowns on their heads. They sit on thrones that surround the throne of God.

Revelation 4:9–12 explains their heavenly responsibilities in detail:

The living creatures kept praising, honoring, and thanking the one who sits on the throne and who lives forever and ever. At the same time the 24 elders knelt down before the one sitting on the throne. And as they worshiped the one who lives forever, they placed their crowns in front of the throne and said,

> *"Our Lord and God,*
> *you are worthy*
> *to receive glory,*
> *honor, and power.*
> *You created all things,*
> *and by your decision they are*
> *and were created."*

In Revelation 5, the four creatures and twenty-four elders are equipped with harps and gold bowls filled with incense. Though their appearances are strikingly different, their work remains the same. They lead all of heaven in worshiping God.

Seraphim Purifying the Lips of Isaiah
Fresco, Catalan School, Barcelona, Spain (12th century)

THE FAITHFUL ONES

LOOKING FOR GOD BEFORE THE TIME OF CHRIST

Jesus didn't mince his words.

"I am the way, the truth, and the life! . . . Without me, no one can go to the Father" (John 14:6).

The implications of those two sentences for everyone born on the AD side of history are enormous. (For more on those implications, take a look at chapter 4.)

But what about the BC folk? What happened to the faithful people of God who lived and died before Jesus came to earth?

According to Scripture, they are enjoying God's presence—for eternity.

Faith is the key. Abram (better known as Abraham) had it. *"Abram believed the LORD, so the LORD was pleased with him and accepted him"* (Genesis 15:6).

Job had it. Even in the depths of his suffering, he was able to declare with certainty: *"My flesh may be destroyed, yet from this body I will see God. Yes, I will see him for myself, and I long for that moment"* (Job 19:26–27). Not only did Job maintain his trust in God but he understood that his faith would allow him to experience God's presence after he died.

David had faith too. And he, like Job, understood its eternal significance: *"Your kindness and love will always be with me each day of my life, and I will live forever in your house, LORD"* (Psalm 23:6).

The heaven-bound status of Old Testament saints is treated as a given in the New Testament as well. In Hebrews 11, the writer presented the so-called Faith Hall of Fame—a roster of Old Testament people who demonstrated extraordinary faith. After concluding the list, the writer offered this word of encouragement to believers: *"Such a large crowd of witnesses is all around us! So we must get rid of everything that slows us down, especially the sin that just won't let go. And we must be determined to run the race that is ahead of us"* (Hebrews 12:1).

Like spectators in a stadium, the heroes of the faith are watching our spiritual progress with great interest, cheering us on to the finish line, so that we may receive the eternal rewards they enjoy.

Read It for Yourself
HEBREWS 11:13–16, 39–40

Every one of those people died. But they still had faith, even though they had not received what they had been promised. They were glad just to see these things from far away, and they agreed that they were only strangers and foreigners on this earth. When people talk this way, it is clear they are looking for a place to call their own. If they had been talking about the land where they had once lived, they could have gone back at any time. But they were looking forward to a better home in heaven. This is why God wasn't ashamed for them to call him their God.

He even built a city for them. . . . All of them pleased God because of their faith! But still they died without being given what had been promised. This was because God had something better in store for us. And he did not want them to reach the goal of their faith without us.

But God has promised us a
new heaven and a new earth,
where justice will rule.
We are really looking forward to this!

2 Peter 3:13

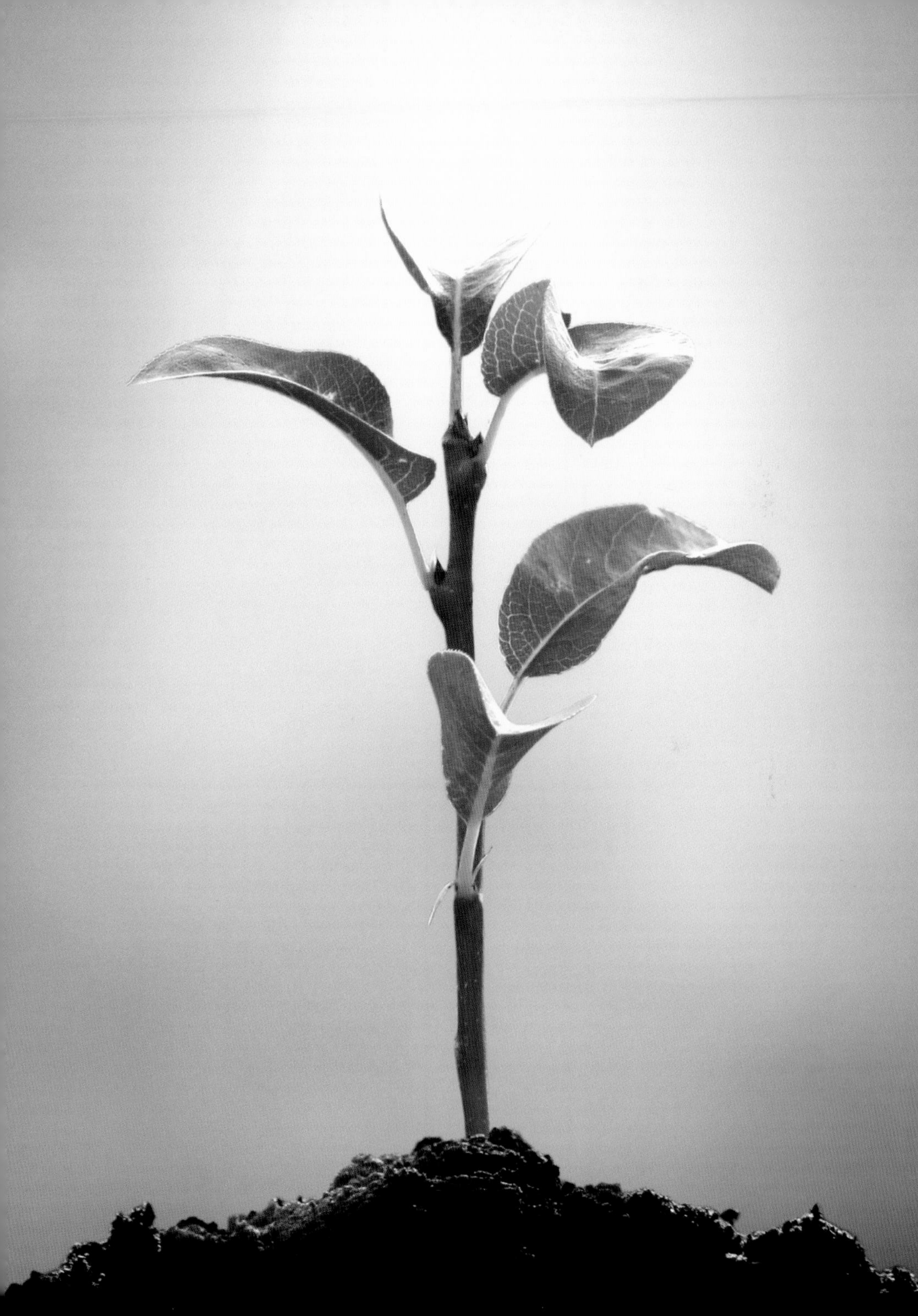

BELIEVERS
BOUND FOR GLORY

God's home is now with his people. He will live with them, and they will be his own. Yes, God will make his home among his people. He will wipe all tears from their eyes, and there will be no more death, suffering, crying, or pain. These things of the past are gone forever. (Revelation 21:3b–4)

Who are these people—these blessed individuals who will live with God forever and enjoy the unimaginable benefits that go with it?

Scripturally speaking, they are the ones whose names are found written in the book of life (Revelation 3:5; 20:15; 21:27). They are the ones who, as the apostle Paul taught, believe in the Lord Jesus (Acts 16:31). They are the ones who acknowledge that Jesus alone is the way, the truth, and the life—and that no one may experience God's presence except through him (John 14:6).

Among them will be some of the best the human race has to offer:

- Humble people who brought glory to God in every situation
- Selfless individuals who put others' needs ahead of their own
- Inspiring men, women, and children who—through pain, suffering, and physical limitations—persevered without losing their spiritual perspective
- Difference makers who were instrumental in leading other people to Jesus

And standing shoulder-to-shoulder with those spiritual heroes will be some of the worst people who ever lived:

- Parents who mistreated their children
- Slave owners
- Swindlers and con artists
- Drug traffickers
- Murderers

Mixed in among those two extremes will be countless "regular" folks who neither rose to dizzying spiritual heights nor sank to the depths of moral depravity.

What could such a wildly disparate group of individuals have in common? At some point in their lives, all of them recognized their sinfulness and asked God for forgiveness. They trusted Jesus to save them from the punishment for their sins.

And, according to God's Word, anyone else who does the same will join them in his presence forever.

Christ Glorified in the Center of Heaven (detail), Fra Angelico (c. 1395–1455)

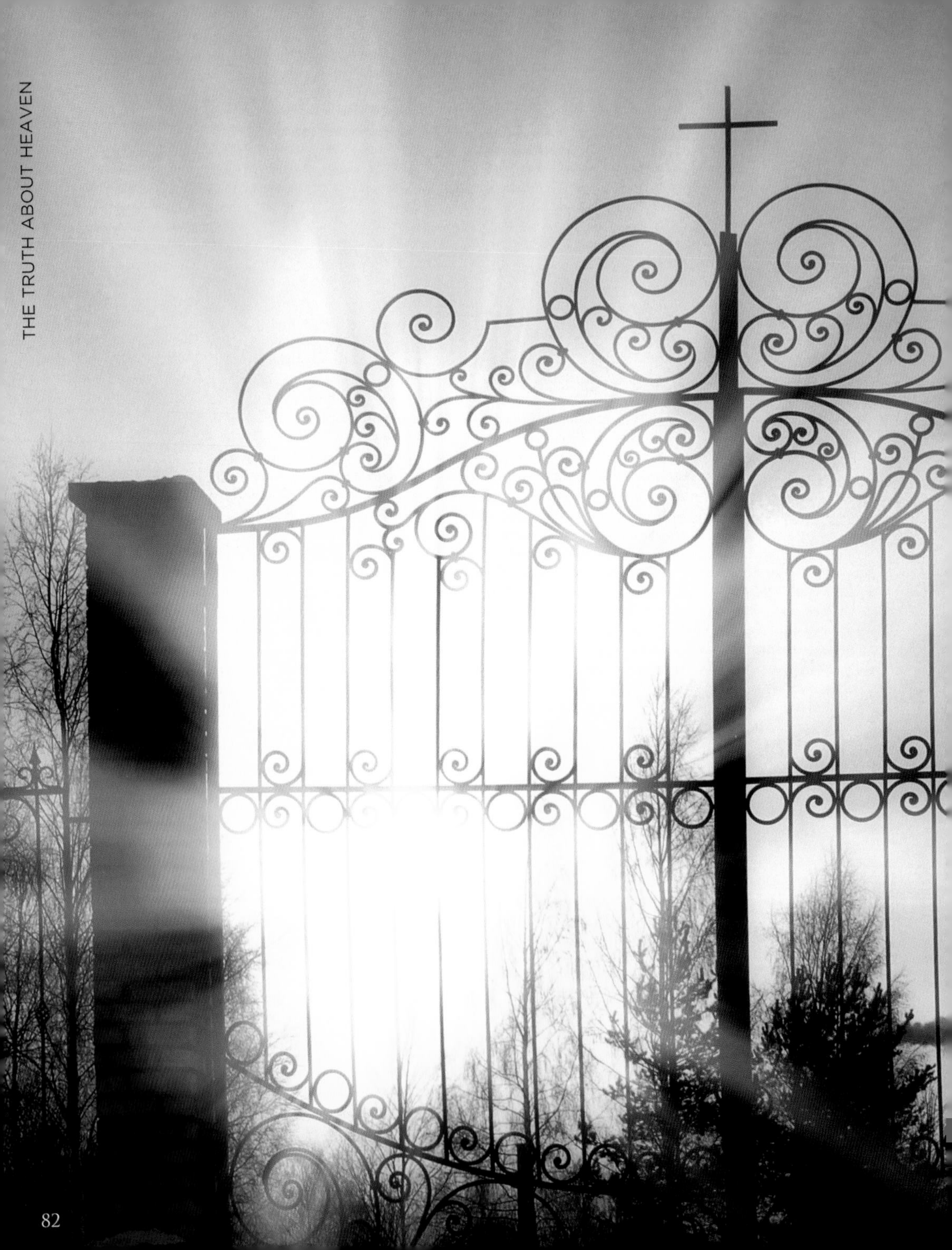

Then the king will say to those on his right, "My father has blessed you! Come and receive the kingdom that was prepared for you before the world was created."

Matthew 25:34

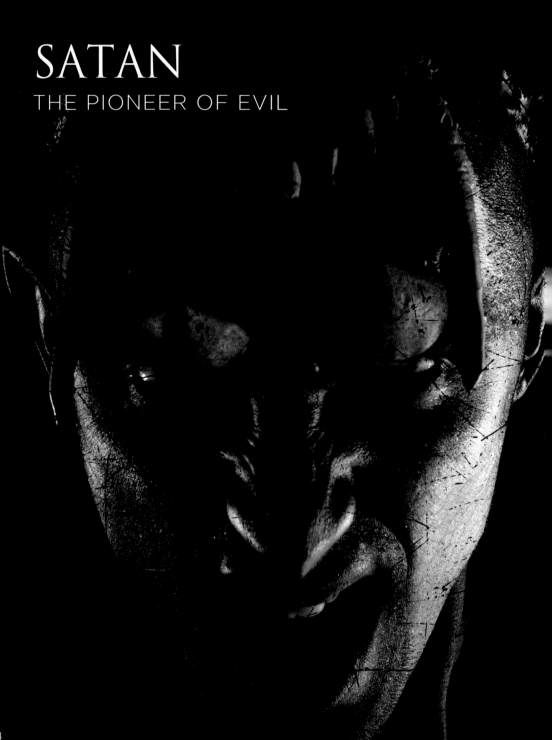

SATAN
THE PIONEER OF EVIL

Quick, name the created being God called *"perfect, intelligent, and good-looking"* (Ezekiel 28:12), and *"bright morning star"* (Isaiah 14:12).

If you guessed *Satan*, congratulations. You know more about the devil, or Lucifer as he's also called, than most people.

Throughout the centuries, many artists and writers have found the descriptions of the devil's outer beauty to be too much at odds with his inner evil. As a result, his depictions have devolved into broad caricatures of evil. The radiant angel of light has become a red-horned, cloven-hooved, pointy-tailed monster—the fire-loving king of hell who cackles maniacally at the suffering of those whose souls he has claimed.

The danger of trafficking in such cartoonish images is that it blinds people to Satan's actual nature and work.

Who is Satan, really? According to the Bible, he

- led a rebellion against God and was kicked out of heaven;
- tempted Eve to disobey God in the Garden of Eden, causing both her and Adam to bring sin into the world;
- tempted Jesus to sin, but failed miserably;
- established himself as the chief adversary of God, his people, and his plan.

He's a dangerous enemy, to be sure. First Peter 5:8 describes him as *"a roaring lion, sneaking around to find someone to attack."* Yet his cause is ultimately futile. He still fights battles, but he has lost the war. And his fate is sealed.

"Then the devil who fooled them will be thrown into the lake of fire and burning sulfur. He will be there with the beast and the false prophet, and they will be in pain day and night forever and ever" (Revelation 20:10).

The subject of Ezekiel 28 is identified as the king of Tyre. The subject of Isaiah 14 is identified as the king of Babylon. However, many Bible scholars believe that their stories parallel the fall of Satan and that the words addressed to them also apply to him.

DEMONS
WHEN ANGELS GO BAD

If pop culture has taught us anything, it's that a demon's chief responsibility is to appear suddenly, in miniaturized form, on the left shoulder of a person who's facing temptation. The demon's job is to counter the influence of the goody-goody angel who has suddenly appeared on the person's right shoulder.

For reasons as yet unexplained by theologians, the demon looks exactly like the person being tempted; wears devil's horns, a red unitard, and a cape; carries a pitchfork; and vanishes in a puff of smoke when the temptation is resisted.

How such a benign caricature came to represent such a malevolent being is anyone's guess. The Bible, however, presents a much darker depiction of demons, including their origin, work, and ultimate fate.

According to Revelation 12, when the angel Satan launched his rebellion against God, one-third of the angels in heaven joined him. Their uprising was short-lived. God threw the insurgents out of heaven and forced them to dwell as spirits in the realm between earth and hell. Those rebellious angels are the beings we know as demons.

Beaten but unbowed, the demons shifted their attention to God's human creation. They set about thwarting the Creator's plan for humanity and disrupting his work in the world. A demon's primary aim is to oppress God's people. In extreme cases, a demon may possess a person's body and exercise a certain measure of control over the person's actions.

Though demons have long been the stuff of nightmares, their power is quite limited. They are helpless in the face of God's might. Jesus demonstrated this time and again during his earthly ministry. He drove demons out of an untold number of people, including Mary Magdalene, who became one of his most trusted followers (Luke 8:1–2).

Demons continue their evil work today. Their tools are temptation, doubt, egotism, fear, prejudice, laziness, pride, greed, jealousy—anything that might interfere in our relationship with God or neutralize our work for him. And they are relentless in their attacks.

Such malevolence will not go unpunished forever, though. Passages such as Jude 6 and Revelation 20:7–14 point to a time of reckoning, a day of judgment, for demons. Jesus spoke of an *"everlasting fire prepared for the devil and his angels"* (Matthew 25:41). There, the tormenters will become the tormented.

Read It for Yourself

REVELATION 12:1–6

Something important appeared in the sky. It was a woman whose clothes were the sun. The moon was under her feet, and a crown made of twelve stars was on her head. She was about to give birth, and she was crying because of the great pain.

Something else appeared in the sky. It was a huge red dragon with seven heads and ten horns, and a crown on each of its seven heads. With its tail, it dragged a third of the stars from the sky and threw them down to the earth. Then the dragon turned toward the woman, because it wanted to eat her child as soon as it was born.

The woman gave birth to a son, who would rule all nations with an iron rod. The boy was snatched away. He was taken to God and placed on his throne. The woman ran into the desert to a place that God had prepared for her. There she would be taken care of for 1,260 days.

THE ANTICHRIST AND HIS MINIONS

The antichrist—or beast, as he is also known—figures prominently in just a handful of chapters in the book of Revelation. (He's also referred to occasionally elsewhere in Scripture.) Some biblical scholars generally identify the first beast from the sea (Revelation 13:1; see also Daniel 7:2–4) with the Roman Empire, particularly with Emperor Nero and his persecution of early Christian believers.

Despite his limited biblical coverage, the antichrist has successfully emerged as a bad guy for the ages. He is featured prominently in dozens of movies (most notably, *The Omen* trilogy) and hundreds of novels and songs (most of them in the heavy metal genre). What is it about this figure that inspires such infamy?

The obvious draw is the name. If you're an author looking for the ultimate villain or symbol for evil, why wouldn't you choose the one whose very moniker announces an opposition to Jesus and everything he stands for?

The antichrist of Scripture certainly lives up to his name. The apostle Paul warned, *"When the wicked one appears, Satan will pretend to work all kinds of miracles, wonders, and signs. Lost people will be fooled by his evil deeds. They could be saved, but they will refuse to love the truth and accept it"* (2 Thessalonians 2:9–10).

Revelation 13 portrays the antichrist as a political and spiritual manipulator—a powerful figure whose purpose is to oppose God and make life miserable for those who align themselves with God. Trickery and persecution are the tools of his trade. The antichrist is assisted in his evil work by a figure known as the "false prophet"—a malevolent cheerleader of sorts who encourages and intimidates people into worshiping the antichrist.

For a season, the antichrist, the false prophet, and their followers succeed in their efforts. But that season is followed by a reckoning. Such brazen opposition and blasphemy will not—cannot—go unpunished, as Revelation 19:20 so graphically attests:

> *But the beast was captured and so was the false prophet. This is the same prophet who had worked miracles for the beast, so he could fool everyone who had the mark of the beast and worshiped the idol. The beast and the false prophet were thrown alive into a lake of burning sulfur.*

The Christian Martyrs' Last Prayer
Jean-Léon Gérôme (1824–1900)

2 THESSALONIANS
2:1-12

When our Lord Jesus returns, we will be gathered up to meet him. So I ask you, my friends, not to be easily upset or disturbed by people who claim the Lord has already come. They may say they heard this directly from the Holy Spirit, or from someone else, or even that they read it in one of our letters. But don't be fooled! People will rebel against God. Then before the Lord returns, the wicked one who is doomed to be destroyed will appear. He will brag and oppose everything holy or sacred. He will even sit in God's temple and claim to be God. Don't you remember I told you this while I was still with you?

You already know what is holding this wicked one back until it is time for him to come. His mysterious power is already at work, but someone is holding him back. And the wicked one won't appear until this someone is out of the way. Then he will appear, but the Lord Jesus will kill him simply by breathing on him. He will be completely destroyed by the Lord's glorious return.

When the wicked one appears, Satan will pretend to work all kinds of miracles, wonders, and signs. Lost people will be fooled by his evil deeds. They could be saved, but they will refuse to love the truth and accept it. So God will make sure they are fooled into believing a lie. All of them will be punished, because they would rather do evil than believe the truth.

UNBELIEVERS
NAMES NOT FOUND

Revelation 20:15 is a stark reminder that not everyone chooses to accept God's gift of eternal life through his Son. Some people exercise their God-given free will to reject the Lord and everything he stands for.

The dark side of free will is that it allows us to make stunningly bad decisions—choices we will regret now and possibly forever. Free will means we have a choice, and every choice we make carries with it a consequence. Some consequences are good; some are bad. And some are *tragic*. The consequence of rejecting Jesus falls squarely in the third category.

According to the apostle Paul, those who opt to live apart from Christ will be punished with *"eternal destruction, and they will be kept far from the presence of our Lord and his glorious strength"* (2 Thessalonians 1:9).

Even more heart-wrenching is the fact that many won't see their final fate coming. Jesus said, *"Not everyone who calls me their Lord will get into the kingdom of heaven"* (Matthew 7:21a). Deluded by self-righteousness, people will seek out false teachers who promise them entrance into heaven by other means. Or they will rely on their own good works to earn God's favor. And they will be bitterly disappointed.

The prospect of spending eternity in hell, apart from God's presence, inspires different reactions in unbelievers. Some see it as an opportunity to challenge the fairness of God's plan. Others question God's nature. (For a more detailed explanation as well as biblical points to counter these objections, check out chapter 4.)

Believers, on the other hand, use it as motivation to save others from suffering that unthinkable fate. The specter of eternal separation from God is the engine that powers evangelical Christianity. Jesus told his followers, *"Go and preach the good news to everyone in the world. Anyone who believes me and is baptized will be saved. But anyone who refuses to believe me will be condemned"* (Mark 16:15–16). Bible passages such as this one have inspired fervent efforts to reach out to unbelievers, to bring them to Christ before they die.

Detail in the Duomo, Florence, Italy

Read It for Yourself

REVELATION 20:11–15

I saw a great white throne with someone sitting on it. Earth and heaven tried to run away, but there was no place for them to go. I also saw all the dead people standing in front of that throne. Every one of them was there, no matter who they had once been. Several books were opened, and then the book of life was opened. The dead were judged by what those books said they had done.

The sea gave up the dead people who were in it, and death and its kingdom also gave up their dead. Then everyone was judged by what they had done. Afterwards, death and its kingdom were thrown into the lake of fire. This is the second death. Anyone whose name wasn't written in the book of life was thrown into the lake of fire.

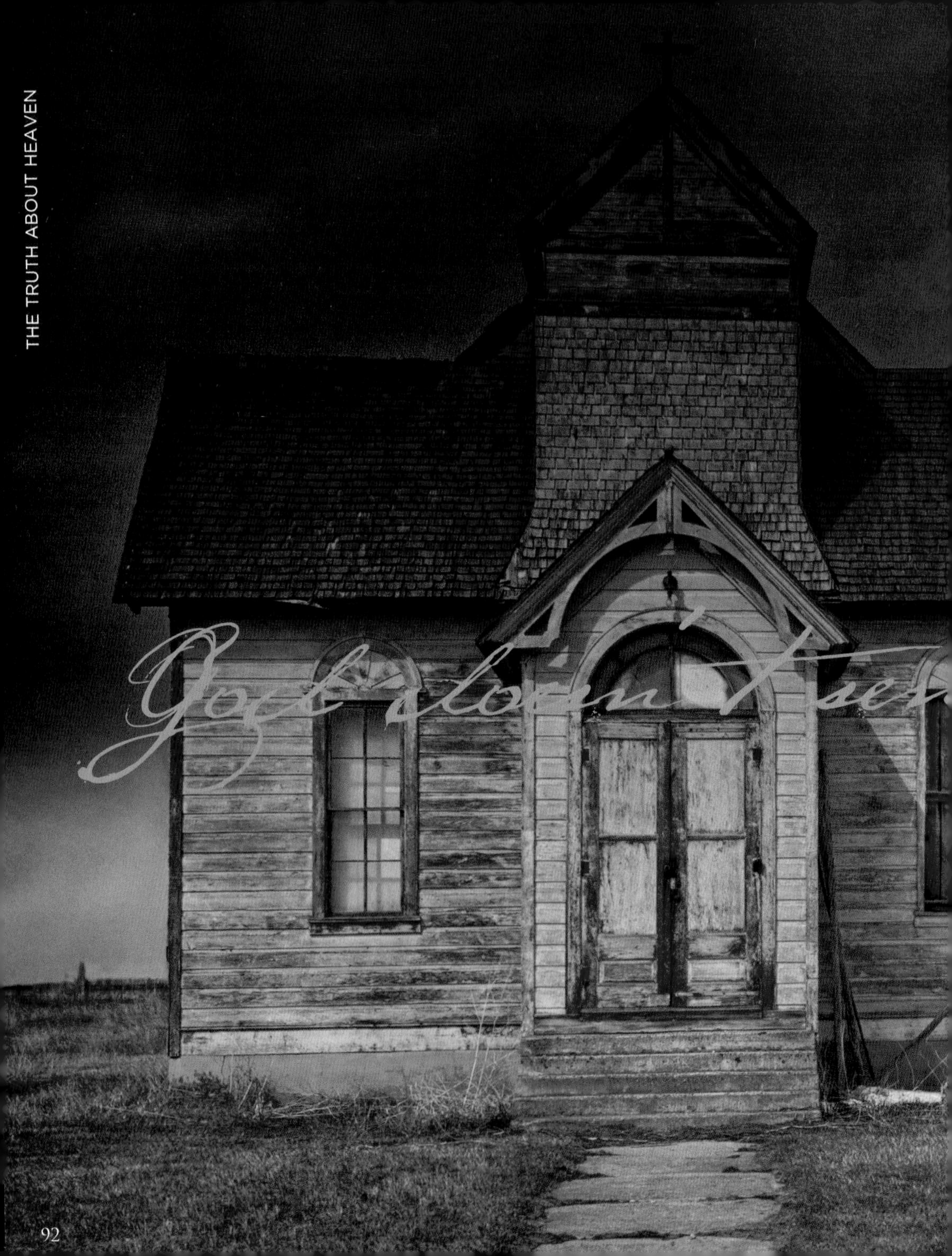

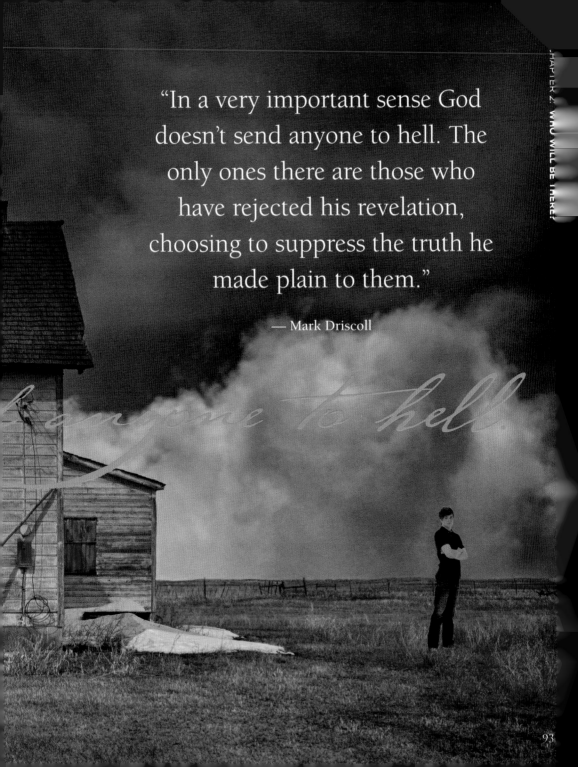

"In a very important sense God doesn't send anyone to hell. The only ones there are those who have rejected his revelation, choosing to suppress the truth he made plain to them."

— Mark Driscoll

"God . . . puts questions in our minds about the past and the future" (Ecclesiastes 3:11).

Our Creator has given each of us an innate awareness that something exists beyond this world. Something good. Something extraordinary. Something that transcends even our imaginations.

The psalmist expressed that awareness as a yearning for God's presence: *"As a deer gets thirsty for streams of water, I truly am thirsty for you, my God. In my heart, I am thirsty for you, the living God. When will I see your face?"* (Psalm 42:1–2).

Something deep inside of us knows that God's presence is the only place where we can truly find what our hearts are longing for: joy, comfort, meaning, security, healing, and fulfillment.

And since heaven is the ultimate experience of God's presence, we are naturally drawn to the idea of eternity.

The good news is we don't have to wait for eternity to experience his presence. God graciously offers us countless "brushes with his deity" and sneak peeks of heavenly realities—here and now.

CHAPTER 3
A TASTE OF HEAVEN

First, there are *theophanies*, God's recorded appearances on earth. These appearances usually occur during times of great opportunity or turmoil. Theophanies are found in the following stories and accounts in Scripture:

- Moses and the burning bush
- The pillars of cloud and fire in the wilderness
- The Law given on Mount Sinai
- The sacred tent (tabernacle)
- The sacred box (ark of the covenant)
- The Jerusalem temple
- Elijah and the whisper
- Isaiah's vision of heaven's throne room
- Ezekiel's vision of the burning amber man
- Jesus' earthly ministry
- The Holy Spirit's work in believers

We get a glimpse of God's presence—and learn something vital about him—in each of these biblical accounts.

Beyond that, God allows us to experience his presence for ourselves in certain areas of daily life:

- Worship
- Fellowship
- Feelings of thankfulness and gratitude
- Appreciation of the beauty of nature
- Enjoyment of the creativity that surrounds us
- Personal experiences of God's nearness

And because God's presence is the essence of heaven, each of these experiences offers tantalizing clues about our eternal home.

ENCOUNTER WITH A SHRUB

Perhaps no one in the Old Testament encountered representations of God's physical, tangible presence more often than Moses. The leader of the Hebrew (Israelite) people enjoyed a unique relationship with the Lord—one that involved direct, person-to-deity interaction.

Though their relationship was close, it was anything but casual. Moses had to follow certain protocol *to the letter* in order to enter God's presence. That pattern was established in Moses' first encounter with God, as recorded in Exodus 3.

Moses was on the lam at the time, a fugitive from Egypt, where he once enjoyed wealth and prestige as the adopted grandson of Pharaoh. His life of privilege came to an abrupt end one day when he spotted an Egyptian beating a Hebrew slave. Moses killed the Egyptian, fled to Midian, married a woman named Zipporah, and started his new life as a shepherd.

One day while he was tending to his flocks, Moses noticed a burning bush—not an unusual sight in the arid climate of Midian. The curious thing was that this particular bush wasn't burning up. The fire wasn't consuming it.

As Moses approached the fiery shrub for a closer look, a voice from within it called him by name and issued a stern warning: *"Don't come any closer. Take off your sandals— the ground where you are standing is holy"* (Exodus 3:5).

Understandably shaken, Moses not only took off his sandals but he also hid his face. He instinctively realized that looking directly at a representation of the holy God was a bad idea.

Wise fellow, that Moses.

He was given an up-close-and-personal glimpse of God's holiness, and it nearly overwhelmed him. He realized that his only course of action was to obey. God gave him instructions to follow, and he followed them.

Thus was born one of the most extraordinary relationships in the Old Testament—a relationship built on Moses' adherence to God's commands. God called him to return to Egypt, confront Pharaoh, and demand the release of the Hebrew slaves. Once the release had been secured, Moses was to lead the entire Hebrew population across the desert wilderness to a land of their own.

Moses had questions and reservations, and he wasn't afraid to communicate these to God. Moses said, *"I will tell the people of Israel that the God their ancestors worshiped has sent me to them. But what should I say, if they ask me your name?"* (Exodus 3:13).

God's response gave Moses all the reassurance he would need: *"I am the eternal God. So tell them that the LORD, whose name is 'I Am,' has sent you. This is my name forever, and it is the name that people must use from now on"* (Exodus 3:14–15).

Moses was able to speak with authority on behalf of I AM because he had been called personally by him and had a relationship with him.

Like every other person, Moses was nowhere near perfect—he hesitated in following God's instructions to lead the Hebrews; an act of disobedience kept him from entering the promised land (see Numbers 20:1–12)—yet his faith in God led to a close relationship with God. Knowing that God used someone like Moses to serve such a great purpose is an inspiration to the rest of us flawed human beings. God can, and will, use us even if we don't deserve it, even if we question God about it, or even if we fight it.

WALK THIS WAY

The Hebrew (Israelite) people were refugees. They had been freed from slavery in Egypt amid the chaos and upheaval of the ten plagues. They had narrowly escaped Pharaoh and his army (thanks to God's intervention) by walking through the Red Sea's parted waters on dry ground.

Their future looked uncertain, to say the least. They were camped at the edge of a desert wilderness with very little food or water. Urging them on was a man who had grown up in Pharaoh's household and later spent years as a fugitive after committing murder in Egypt. He claimed to speak for God, this Moses fellow, though sometimes he got tongue-tied and appointed his brother Aaron to speak for him. They claimed to be leading the Hebrew people to a land the God of Israel had promised their ancestors—a land none of them had ever seen.

Any Hebrew who wasn't ambivalent about what lay ahead wasn't paying attention. The desert wilderness that stretched from horizon to horizon was so foreboding that many in the group saw it as certain death.

What could possibly coax an entire nation of people into such an inhospitable climate?

"During the day the LORD *went ahead of his people in a thick cloud, and during the night he went ahead of them in a flaming fire. That way the* LORD *could lead them at all times, whether day or night"* (Exodus 13:21–22).

God didn't wave good-bye and say, "Good luck with the trip. If you need me, call me." He said, "Here I am. Stay with me. Where I go, you go."

God's presence makes even the scariest journey bearable. And since the Hebrew people needed all the reassurance they could get, he made his presence known in unmistakable ways. Any sudden jolt of panic, doubt, or uncertainty would now be quieted with a mere glance at the ever-present pillar of cloud or fire.

The Israelites Leaving Egypt, c. 1830
David Roberts (1796–1864)

After the king had finally let the people go, the Lord did not lead them through Philistine territory, though that was the shortest way. God had said, "If they are attacked, they may decide to return to Egypt." So he led them around through the desert and toward the Red Sea.

Exodus 13:17–18

"To make the best use of your life, you must never forget two truths:
First, compared with eternity, life is extremely brief.
Second, earth is only a temporary residence. You won't be here long, so don't get too attached. . . .
This is not your permanent home or final destination. You're just passing through, just visiting earth."

— Rick Warren, *The Purpose Driven Life: What on Earth Am I Here For?*

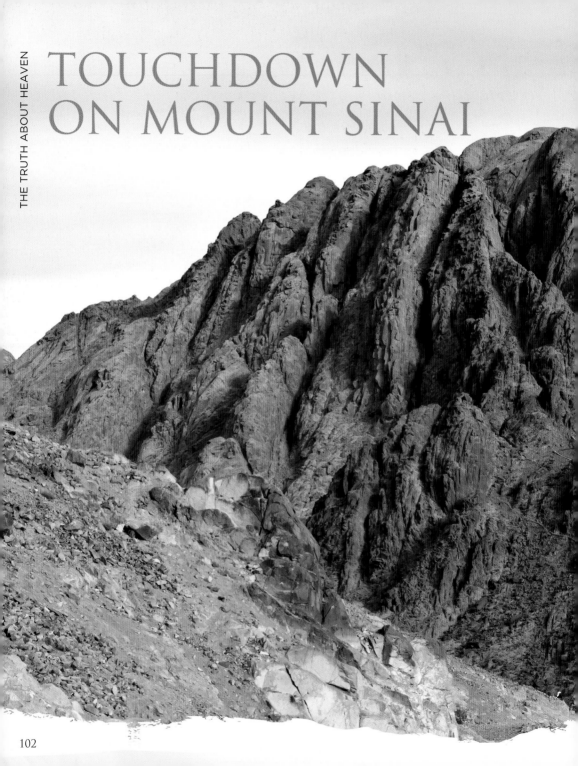

TOUCHDOWN ON MOUNT SINAI

The Hebrews (Israelites) were no strangers to God's incredible power. Before and after the Exodus they witnessed miraculous events such as

- the Nile River turning to blood;
- three days of darkness that covered the Egyptians;
- the death of every firstborn son in Egypt;
- the parting of the waters of the Red Sea;
- water pouring from a rock.

For a group of people who had been given a front-row seat to God's powerful acts in delivering them from the Egyptians, the Hebrews were fairly cavalier in their relationship with the Almighty. They complained about being hungry or thirsty—and then whined about the food he sent from heaven.

By the time they reached Mount Sinai, God had had enough. For their own sake, the Hebrews needed a reminder of who they were dealing with. They needed to understand whose presence was in the pillars of cloud and fire. They needed ground rules. They needed to understand exactly why they had to obey God's instructions.

They needed a reminder of his power—one they would never forget. And that's exactly what they got.

> On the morning of the third day there was thunder and lightning. A thick cloud covered the mountain, a loud trumpet blast was heard, and everyone in camp trembled with fear. Moses led them out of the camp to meet God, and they stood at the foot of the mountain.
>
> Mount Sinai was covered with smoke because the LORD had come down in a flaming fire. Smoke poured out of the mountain just like a furnace, and the whole mountain shook. The trumpet blew louder and louder. Moses spoke, and God answered him with thunder. (Exodus 19:16–19)

As far as we know, this glimpse of God's awe-inspiring power and holiness was something only the angels had witnessed before. For the Hebrew people gathered at the base of the mountain, the experience was both terrifying and reassuring: terrifying because of the unimaginable power on display; reassuring because God's power was on their side.

THE TABERNACLE YEARS

Mishkan (Tabernacle) in Sinai Desert, Balage Balogh

Extraordinary circumstances call for extraordinary measures. The Hebrew people faced an arduous journey across the desert wilderness to the promised land. To help facilitate the trip, God proposed a plan whereby his presence would accompany the people—not some distance ahead of them, as in the cloud or pillar of fire he had faithfully provided since they left Egypt, but *in their midst.*

God proposed to dwell with his people.

In order for that to happen, a set of exacting requirements needed to be met. God gave Moses detailed plans for the construction of the sacred tent (also known as the tabernacle)—a portable structure that would represent the Lord's presence among the Hebrews.

The materials for the sanctuary and its furnishings— including gold, silver, bronze, colored thread, fine linen, goat hair, ram skins, goatskin, leather, and assorted gemstones—were collected from the Hebrew people, who were only too happy to contribute to the cause. The design and construction were entrusted to master craftsmen.

The tabernacle was made up of three sections. The outer courtyard measured 150 feet by 30 feet; its perimeter was lined with 360 feet of fine linen curtains. A basin and bronze altar were set up in the courtyard. The holy place was a 30' x 15' tent inside the courtyard that contained a table, a lampstand, and a gold altar. The most holy place was a 15' x 15' inner sanctum set off from the holy place by a thick curtain. Inside the most holy place was the sacred chest (ark of the covenant), which held the two stone tablets on which the Ten Commandments were inscribed.

The tabernacle became the center of activity for the Hebrew people. When they were on the move, the sacred tent was carried at the front of the procession. When they stopped, their camp was set up around it. The people gathered together at the tabernacle to worship God and offer sacrifices to him. Undoubtedly, many came simply to experience the Lord's closeness.

From within that tabernacle, God's presence accompanied the Hebrew people across the wilderness and into the promised land.

THE SACRED CHEST

The centerpiece of the Hebrew tabernacle—the sacred tent where God interacted with his people—was the sacred chest (also known as the ark of the covenant). When we trace the chest's role in Old Testament history, it's easy to see why George Lucas and Steven Spielberg built the plot of the first *Indiana Jones* movie around it.

The chest, as God envisioned it, was made of acacia wood and covered with gold. Gold rings were fixed to its sides, through which gold-covered poles could be inserted for carrying it. The lid featured sculptures of two golden cherubim—winged creatures—facing one another, their wings touching over their heads. The two stone tablets that contained the inscriptions of the Ten Commandments were placed inside the chest.

The importance of the chest to the Hebrew (Israelite) people cannot be overstated. The tabernacle represented the dwelling place of God among his people, and the chest (specifically, the area between the two cherubim on the lid) represented his throne, the very epicenter of his presence.

The chest led the Hebrew people on their journey through the wilderness. In Exodus 23:27, we find God's explanation regarding the impact his presence would have: *"I will terrify those nations and make your enemies so confused that they will run from you."*

The chest was used to bring down the impenetrable walls of Jericho. The Philistines, bitter enemies of the Hebrews, cowered in the chest's presence but managed to capture it during a particularly brutal battle. When they took it back to their cities, however, plagues broke out. They had no choice but to return the chest to the Hebrews.

God's presence remained with the Hebrew people throughout their wilderness journey and their settlement of the promised land. The chest was kept in the town of Kiriath-Jearim until King David proposed to build a temple to God in Jerusalem. At that point, the chest was transported to Jerusalem amid great celebration.

The sacred chest served as the centerpiece of the Jerusalem temple until the building was destroyed by the Babylonians in 586 BC. After the temple's destruction, the chest, having fulfilled its purpose, was lost to history. Its whereabouts remain unknown.

Moses and Joshua in the Tabernacle, c. 1896–1902
James Jacques Joseph Tissot (1836–1902)

God's presence in the sacred chest was not something to be taken lightly. After the Philistines returned the chest, curiosity got the better of some of the men. They gazed at the sacred chest a little too closely—or perhaps without proper reverence—and were struck dead by God (1 Samuel 6:19–21). Later, while the chest was being carried to Jerusalem, a man named Uzzah reached out to keep it from slipping and was struck dead by God (2 Samuel 6:1–7).

Solomon's temple served as the center of Jewish worship for almost 400 years, from its dedication (circa 960 BC) until its destruction by the Babylonians in 586 BC.

A PLACE
IN JERUSALEM

King David had a dream, a fervent desire, really, to build a temple in Jerusalem—not just any temple, but the grandest, most glorious temple ever constructed. He desired to build a temple that would bring honor to the Lord God of Israel and give his people a place to worship him.

Unfortunately, David's dream remained unfulfilled during his lifetime. As a warrior king, he had spilled blood in his conquest of the promised land. In God's eyes, that made him an unsuitable candidate for building his temple. So David had to content himself with overseeing the preparations for construction. He moved the sacred chest, the centerpiece of the temple, to Jerusalem. He purchased the land on which the temple would be built. He assembled the labor force. He gathered the building materials.

But the privilege of building the temple would fall to King Solomon, David's son. David's close ally, King Hiram of Tyre, agreed to provide the wood and skilled woodworkers for the project. Solomon supplemented their numbers with thirty thousand additional laborers.

Even with such a workforce, the construction took seven years to complete. Only the best materials were used. And the results were magnificent.

The primary structure was a massive, oblong sanctuary surrounded by side rooms on several different levels. Those, in turn, were surrounded by cloisters supported by ornate colonnades. The entrance was flanked by two grand pillars.

A series of walled and gated courtyards surrounded the sanctuary, each one designed according to highly detailed specifications. Inside the temple was an inner sanctuary called the most holy place (as it was called in the tabernacle), which housed the sacred chest.

After the temple was completed, Solomon led a solemn dedication ceremony. Prayers were offered. God's covenant with his people was read. His promises were celebrated. Then God filled the temple with smoke—a sign to his people that he would indeed dwell with them.

King Solomon used his vast resources to create a temple to honor God. God not only accepted the king's offering but he also chose to make it his dwelling place in a localized way among his people.

Perhaps better than anyone else, Solomon in his wisdom understood the implications of having God's presence so near. So we'll leave the last words on the subject to him: *"There's not enough room in all of heaven for you, LORD God. How could you possibly live on earth in this temple I have built?"* (1 Kings 8:27).

ELIJAH AND THE GENTLE BREEZE

"Go out and stand on
the mountain," the LORD replied.
"I want you to be there when I
pass by."

All at once, a strong wind shook
the mountain and shattered the rocks.
But the LORD was not in
the wind. Next, there was an
earthquake, but the LORD was
not in the earthquake. Then
there was a fire, but the LORD
was not in the fire.

Finally, there was a gentle
breeze, and when Elijah heard
it, he covered his face with his coat.
He went out and stood at
the entrance to the cave.

1 Kings 19:11–13a

Elijah should have been on top of the world. Thanks to God's intervention, he had single-handedly scored a decisive victory over 850 prophets of Baal and Asherah (1 Kings 18). He had shown the people of Israel that God alone is deity.

Yet Elijah felt alone and scared. The upstaging (and subsequent massacre) of the false prophets landed him on Queen Jezebel's hit list. She and King Ahab responded by unleashing a reign of terror on the prophets of God—terror so intense that only one, Elijah, remained. Everyone else was dead or on the run, or so Elijah believed.

The beleaguered prophet retreated to Mount Sinai. By that time, he was running on fumes and sought God for help. He desperately needed direction, comfort, encouragement, and reassurance.

God was more than happy to oblige. He directed Elijah to a cave and announced that he would make himself known to the prophet, personally. Elijah stood inside the cave and watched as a powerful wind tore the mountains apart and shattered rocks. But God's presence was not in the wind.

The wind was followed by a mighty earthquake. But God's presence wasn't in the earthquake. Then came a roaring fire, but God's presence wasn't in the fire either.

Finally, Elijah felt a gentle breeze. He immediately covered his face with his cloak because he recognized God's presence in the breeze. In that still, small voice, God gave Elijah the encouragement he was looking for.

Through Elijah's plight, God also teaches a valuable lesson to everyone who seeks him. He could have made his presence known in an obvious, show-stopping way— using wind, earthquake, or fire. In this case, though, he chose to make his presence known through a soft, gentle breeze—a gesture of closeness and intimacy.

ISAIAH IN THE THRONE ROOM

Almost 800 years before the Son of Man told the apostle John to write down what he saw in his vision of heaven, the Old Testament prophet Isaiah was given a supernatural peek into God's throne room (see Isaiah 6). What he saw will seem familiar to those who have read the book of Revelation—and exceedingly odd to those who have not.

The defining event that ignited Isaiah's vision was the death of King Uzziah. According to 2 Kings 15:3, Uzziah (also known as Azariah) *"obeyed the LORD by doing right, as his father Amaziah had done."* He led successful military campaigns against the hated Philistines. He was a renowned builder and planner. His fame as a monarch spread as far as Egypt.

His one notable transgression, though, cost him nearly everything. In 2 Chronicles 26:16, we read that King Uzziah, who had become a bit full of himself, entered the temple to burn incense. For his temerity, God struck the king with leprosy, forcing him to live in isolation until his death.

The death of King Uzziah prompted Isaiah to wonder: Where was God in all of this? Why would he allow a good king to face such an ignominious end? What did Uzziah's death mean for Israel? Could the people still trust God to protect, lead, and direct them?

In response, God offered Isaiah much more than reassurance; he gave the prophet an indelible vision of the One who is in absolute control of everything. Everything in Isaiah's vision depicts majesty and royalty, from the awe-inspiring throne to the train of the Almighty's robe that fills the temple to the mighty, flaming winged creatures who offer never-ending praise and service.

God made his presence known to the prophet Isaiah in a dramatic way so that he could, in turn, assure the people of Israel of the absoluteness of the Lord's power and authority.

113

PSALM 23:6

Your kindness and love
will always be with me
each day of my life,
and I will live forever
in your house, LORD.

EZEKIEL AND THE BURNING AMBER MAN

As the son of a priest, Ezekiel had every intention of following in his father's footsteps. He trained and prepared specifically to serve in the temple in Jerusalem. But his plans were thwarted when he and the people of Judah were captured by the Babylonians and taken into exile.

While he was in captivity, Ezekiel received his true call to service. God selected him to serve as a prophet—a spokesman for the Lord and a deliverer of his messages—to the displaced Israelites. God understood that prophesying to the notoriously hard-hearted Israelites was a tough gig. After all, their continual rebellion against him is what caused the whole lot of them to be exiled in the first place. God knew Ezekiel would face rejection and, consequently, wrestle with doubt and discouragement. So before he issued his call, God pulled back the curtain of heaven and gave his servant a peek inside.

Ezekiel watched in amazement as the four creatures described in Revelation 4—the attendants of God's throne—went flying to and fro. He saw an expanse as vast as the horizon glittering like crystal. He saw a throne made of sapphire, and on the throne sat a figure whose appearance resembled a human.

God offered Ezekiel this glimpse of heaven to energize and encourage him—and to inspire urgency in the prophet's words. Having glimpsed the One who had called him, Ezekiel could speak with authority on God's behalf.

Read It for Yourself
EZEKIEL 1:27-28

From the waist up, it was glowing like metal in a hot furnace, and from the waist down it looked like the flames of a fire. The figure was surrounded by a bright light, as colorful as a rainbow that appears after a storm.

I realized I was seeing the brightness of the Lord's glory! So I bowed with my face to the ground, and just then I heard a voice speaking to me.

Jesus Carries His Cross, St. Michael's Church

GOD IN THE FLESH

The most illustrative and informative example of God's presence on earth was a thirty-three-year sojourn by Jesus, God the Son, that began around 4 BC and continued until forty days after his resurrection. During that time, Jesus was fully divine and fully human. Those who encountered him, even merely *touching* him, found themselves in the presence of God, whether they realized it or not.

Trying to encompass the scope of Jesus' words and actions during his time on earth is nearly impossible. Even the Gospel writers struggled with it. The apostle John said, *"Jesus did many other things. If they were all written in books, I don't suppose there would be room enough in the whole world for all the books"* (John 21:25).

During his earthly ministry, though, Jesus did offer us a finite preview of his eternal gift. During his time among us, Jesus used his power over creation to heal—to bring physical, emotional, and spiritual wholeness to people.

He restored broken bodies. He eased troubled minds. He restored equilibrium to lives that had spun out of control.

The Bible records more than two dozen miraculous healings performed by Jesus. He radically changed the lives and bodies of

- deaf people;
- blind people;
- disabled people;
- paralyzed people;
- people who suffered from leprosy;
- people stricken with unnamed illnesses;
- people who were possessed by demons;
- people who had died.

In so doing, Jesus pointed to a future of *hope and redemption* for all who follow him. That is, our bodies will be renewed, transformed, and made ready for eternity in God's presence.

The apostle Paul described it this way:

> *That's how it will be when our bodies are raised to life. These bodies will die, but the bodies that are raised will live forever. These ugly and weak bodies will become beautiful and strong. As surely as there are physical bodies, there are spiritual bodies. And our physical bodies will be changed into spiritual bodies.* (1 Corinthians 15:42–44)

In heaven, we will share the joy of being renewed along with those who experienced Jesus' healing words and touch during his time on earth.

Read It for Yourself
JOHN 1:1-3

In the beginning was the one
  who is called the Word.
The Word was with God
  and was truly God.
From the very beginning
  the Word was with God.
And with this Word,
  God created all things.
Nothing was made
  without the Word.

"The doctrine of the Kingdom of Heaven, which was the main teaching of Jesus, is certainly one of the most revolutionary doctrines that ever stirred and changed human thought."

— H. G. Wells, *A Short History of the World*

HOLY SPIRIT

Jesus made no secret of the fact that his time on earth was short—much to his followers' dismay. The disciples were troubled by the prospect of life without him. So Jesus helped them understand that his departure would be offset by a very important arrival, a parting gift, of sorts.

> Then I will ask the Father to send you the Holy Spirit who will help you and always be with you. The Spirit will show you what is true. The people of this world cannot accept the Spirit, because they don't see or know him. But you know the Spirit, who is with you and will keep on living in you. (John 14:16–17)

God's Holy Spirit would take up residence *inside* every believer. What Jesus did through an external relationship with his followers, the Holy Spirit would do through an *internal* one.

What was true for Jesus' first disciples is true for Christians today. Everyone who follows Jesus is a vessel of the Holy Spirit. God's presence—the very essence of heaven—dwells *inside* us.

That doesn't mean that Christians live in a constant heaven-on-earth euphoria. Our imperfect surroundings and circumstances prevent us from experiencing what heaven will really be like. However, God's presence—his Holy Spirit— creates a seismic impact on our lives.

He acts as our spiritual conscience.
The Holy Spirit lets us know when we're doing something wrong and urges us to confess and repent. He encourages us to remove the obstacles that get in the way of our relationship with God.

He translates infinite into finite.
According to 1 Corinthians 2:10–11, the Spirit assists us in understanding the deep things of God. He helps us comprehend Scripture and make sense of divine concepts.

He gives spiritual gifts.
The Holy Spirit equips us for our work on earth. He gives us the necessary tools to carry out God's will for our lives.

God's presence in our lives assists us in navigating this temporary world and gives us a taste of what the next world will be like.

Pentecost, detail from cathedral, Antwerp, Belgium

WE SHOULD
BE CHEERFUL,
BECAUSE
WE WOULD
RATHER LEAVE
THESE BODIES
AND BE AT
HOME WITH
THE LORD.

2 CORINTHIANS 5:8

WORSHIP
HEAVEN'S NATIONAL PASTIME

Tucked into the strange, apocalyptic narrative of the book of Revelation are a few familiar images—snapshots that suggest certain aspects of heaven that bear at least a passing resemblance to aspects of life here on earth. Perhaps the most recognizable illustration of this is in the gathering of believers for worship.

> *Then I heard all beings in heaven and on the earth and under the earth and in the sea offer praise. Together, all of them were saying, "Praise, honor, glory, and strength forever and ever to the one who sits on the throne and to the Lamb!"* (Revelation 5:13)

Certainly the scale of worship in heaven surpasses anything we'll ever experience on earth. Even so, heavenly worship and earthly worship share some important traits.

Both are reactions to God's presence.
The sense we get in Revelation is that the people and angels in heaven are compelled to respond in the only way they know—through worship. As far as they're concerned, the only fitting reaction to such closeness with God is to give him praise and glory. The same holds true for worship on earth. We may not yet have a heavenly vantage point of God's presence, but Jesus has given us this assurance: *"Whenever two or three of you come together in my name, I am there with you"* (Matthew 18:20).

Both celebrate the Lord's perfections.
Revelation 5:12 reveals that the reason the assembled masses of heaven praise the Lord is because he is worthy—worthy to receive power, riches, wisdom, strength, honor, glory, and blessing. The text implies that any one of those elements can—and will—be singled out for further worship. There is no halfhearted praise, no lazy, thank-you-God-for-everything generalities. In the book of Revelation, there is no such thing as apathetic worship among God's people.

Both are greater than the sum of their individual parts.
Something happens when our voices join with like-minded people to give glory and honor to God. We become part of something bigger than ourselves. We create a noise more joyful than anything we could come up with individually.

Corporate worship brings us closer to one another and to God—on earth, as it is in heaven.

> "I can safely say, on the authority of all that is revealed in the Word of God, that any man or woman on this earth who is bored and turned off by worship is not ready for heaven."
>
> A. W. Tozer

From the *Bamberg Apocalypse*, c. 15th century

ALL TOGETHER NOW

Is there a word more exclusively Christian than *fellowship*? Think about it. When was the last time you heard the word used outside of a church context?

- "The police had to break up Kelly's fellowship after the neighbors complained about the noise."
- "If anyone asks for me, tell them I'll be fellowshipping at the beach this afternoon."
- "I don't usually fellowship with coworkers, but I was wondering if you'd like to have dinner with me on Friday."

It's not a word that gets thrown around casually—and perhaps for good reason. The Christian context of the word is profoundly relevant and integral to our identity as followers of Christ. A casual interpretation may simply lose too much in translation.

The apostle John's vision of heaven suggests that fellowship plays a large role in our eternal future. We will join with believers from around the world and across the span of time—celebrating our salvation and worshiping the God who made it possible. Our appreciation of what Christ accomplished will be magnified by joyfully sharing it with others. Our voices will mingle in praise.

We can enjoy a taste of that fellowship in the here and now. As members of the body of Christ, we share a connection based on common beliefs, purposes, and goals. On a deeper level, we are complemented, strengthened, and, to a certain extent, completed by our fellow believers. We share a mutual dependence on one another. When one part of the body suffers, the entire body suffers.

Consider the following passages:

- John 13:34 (love each other)
- 1 Thessalonians 5:14 (warn, encourage, help the weak, be patient)
- Colossians 3:13 (put up with each other, forgive)
- Philippians 2:4 (care about others as much as ourselves)

All these assume personal relationships on the part of believers—relationships marked by love, compassion, encouragement, forgiveness, and accountability. These are the kind of relationships that are built through fellowship. These are the kind of relationships that will last throughout eternity.

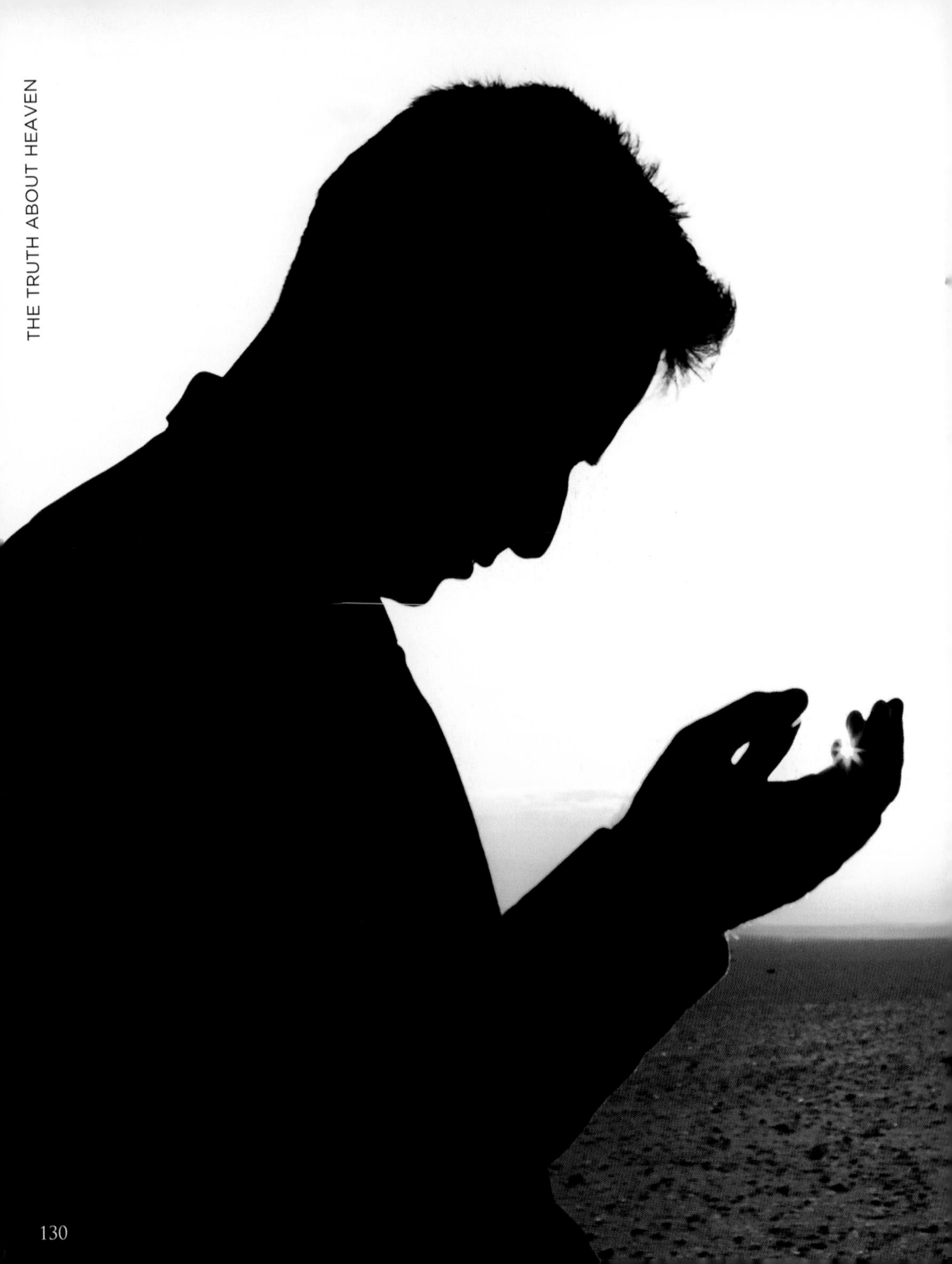

THANK YOU VERY MUCH

Every day is Thanksgiving in heaven.

In heaven, we will finally be set free from the self-centeredness and obliviousness that plague us in this world. We will see clearly and appreciate everything God has done for us. Everything that is unknown to us will be revealed—from the details of our creation to the circumstances of our salvation; from the people he surrounds us with to the countless circumstances he works through.

The results will be as thrilling as they are humbling. Imagine being able to fully comprehend the depth of God's love for us, to clearly see every bit of tangible evidence of that love.

"I don't think you should spend your life praying for things, but I do believe you should thank God for what He's given you . . . but I think the scripture teaches us that we can pray for our dreams, pray for the big things . . . he's not a small God; this God is incredible."

Joel Osteen

Is it any wonder the apostle John's vision of heaven is full of scenes like this one in Revelation 11:16–17:

Then the 24 elders, who were seated on thrones in God's presence, knelt down and worshiped him. They said,

"Lord God All-Powerful,
you are and you were,
and we thank you.
You used your great power
and started ruling."

That attitude of gratitude is the by-product of living in God's presence. The closer we get to him, the more thankful we will be.

Fortunately, for those of us still sojourning in this world, the reverse is also true. The more thankful we are, the closer we get to God. Recognizing and acknowledging what he's done—and what he continues to do on our behalf—strengthens our relationship with him.

"Whatever happens, keep thanking God because of Jesus Christ. This is what God wants you to do" (1 Thessalonians 5:18).

We don't have to wait for eternity to enjoy the benefits of thankfulness. We can develop a heavenly perspective by fostering a spirit of gratitude in our daily lives. The more we recognize and acknowledge God's fingerprints on the good things in our lives, the more joy and contentment we'll experience.

God makes himself known through his creation.
The Old Testament says so.

> *The heavens keep telling*
>   *the wonders of God,*
> *and the skies declare*
>   *what he has done.*
> *Each day informs*
>   *the following day;*
> *each night announces*
>   *to the next.*
> *They don't speak a word,*
> *and there is never*
>   *the sound of a voice.*
> *Yet their message reaches*
>   *all the earth,*
> *and it travels*
>   *around the world.* (Psalm 19:1–4a)

So does the New Testament.

> *God's eternal power and character cannot be seen. But from the*
> *beginning of creation, God has shown what these are like by*
> *all he has made. That's why those people don't have any excuse.*
> (Romans 1:20)

The sheer vastness of the universe reveals God's power. The intricate
design of all living creatures reveals his intelligence. The stunning
variety of flora and fauna reveals his creativity. The fact that
our environment protects and sustains us reveals his care and
compassion.

Therefore it stands to reason that the closer we get to nature, the
more we appreciate the beauty of God's creation. And the more we
appreciate the beauty of God's creation, the closer we get to his
presence. So when poets, songwriters, and state tourism boards talk
about finding a slice of heaven in some geological landmark, they
aren't far off the mark.

The book of Revelation closes with God's creation of a new heaven
and new earth. And what works they will be! We will have eternity
to explore their wonders. In the meantime, we have the here and
now to explore and be awed by his original work.

Want to know God and experience his presence? Study his creation.

IT'S
ONLY
NATURAL

"The most important thing for me is having a relationship with God. To know that the owner, the creator of the universe loves you, sent His Son to die for your sins; that's very empowering. Knowing Him and knowing that He loves me gives me encouragement and confidence to move forward."

Benjamin Carson

AN EYE FOR CREATIVITY

If God is the creative source of everything wondrous and beautiful, and if heaven is the place where God makes his presence known, then it stands to reason that heaven is the pinnacle of creativity, a place of unsurpassed beauty and wonder.

The splendors of heaven certainly pushed the apostle John's creative writing skills to the limit—and beyond. In John's descriptions, we find fantastic (if hard to imagine) examples of God's creativity.

The wall was built of jasper, and the city was made of pure gold, clear as crystal. Each of the twelve foundations was a precious stone. The first was jasper, the second was sapphire, the third was agate, the fourth was emerald, the fifth was onyx, the sixth was carnelian, the seventh was chrysolite, the eighth was beryl, the ninth was topaz, the tenth was chrysoprase, the eleventh was jacinth, and the twelfth was amethyst. Each of the twelve gates was a solid pearl. The streets of the city were made of pure gold, clear as crystal. (Revelation 21:18–21)

The angel showed me a river that was crystal clear, and its waters gave life. The river came from the throne where God and the Lamb were seated. Then it flowed down the middle of the city's main street. On each side of the river are trees that grow a different kind of fruit each month of the year. The fruit gives life, and the leaves are used as medicine to heal the nations. (Revelation 22:1–2)

Heaven, of course, is not the only place where creativity abounds. Where there is humankind, there is the handiwork of artists and artisans. The world's greatest creative endeavors, from creation to present day, are available to us on the walls of museums, in the pages of books, on stages, on screens, or in the designs of architectural marvels—preserved and presented so that we may celebrate that creativity, embrace our God-given identity, and draw closer to the source of it all.

According to Genesis 1:27, humans are made in the image of God, the Creator. Creativity is embedded in our core. When we express our creative impulses, or find something worthwhile in the creativity of others (such as writing, drawing, painting, sculpting, or performing), we are celebrating our unique design.

Whether we realize it or not, we're also adopting a heavenly mind-set. Heaven, after all, is where creativity reaches its zenith.

Read It for Yourself
PSALM 136:1–9

Praise the LORD! He is good.
  God's love never fails.
Praise the God of all gods.
  God's love never fails.
Praise the Lord of lords.
  God's love never fails.
Only God works great miracles.
  God's love never fails.
With wisdom he made the sky.
  God's love never fails.
The Lord stretched the earth
over the ocean.
  God's love never fails.
He made the bright lights
in the sky.
  God's love never fails.
He lets the sun rule each day.
  God's love never fails.
He lets the moon and the stars
rule each night.
  God's love never fails.

IT'S PERSONAL

Some of our encounters with God's presence in this world are as unique and individual as DNA. That shouldn't surprise us. According to Luke 12:7, God knows the exact number of hairs on our heads. It is therefore no stretch to assume that he also knows how to maximize the experiences of his presence in our everyday lives.

Some of these experiences have universal application and lend themselves to dramatic retellings. The most compelling accounts usually make their way into sermon illustrations or social media posts. Other experiences are so idiosyncratic—and occur so deep within us—they defy explanation. But that makes them no less real.

God makes his presence known in an infinite variety of ways, each one perfectly appropriate and customized for the situation at hand. We've all had "divine interventions"—experiences that can only be explained as God's supernatural work. Whether it's a Bible verse that jumps out at us or a well-timed word of encouragement from a friend, God finds ways to let us know we aren't alone.

Below are just a few of the strategies God employs to make his presence known in our lives.

Answered Prayers

Sometimes God makes his presence known by giving us exactly what we ask for and then leaving his fingerprints all over the situation so that there's no mistaking his intervention in our lives.

Unanswered Prayers

Sometimes he makes his presence known by refusing to give us the desires of our hearts and then showing us what would have happened if we had gotten what we wanted.

Calming Spirit

Sometimes God makes his presence known by easing our anxieties and giving us a sense of comfort or calm when, logically, there should be none.

Every one of those experiences is God's way of showing us a little slice of heaven. Remember, heaven is the inevitable result of God's presence. When he makes his presence known in our lives, he gives us a sneak peek into eternity. From his throne in heaven, God bridges the gap between *there* and *here*—and between him and us.

"The function of prayer is not to influence God, but rather to change the nature of the one who prays."

Søren Kierkegaard

Read It for Yourself
MATTHEW 7:7-8

Ask, and you will receive. Search, and
you will find. Knock, and the door will
be opened for you. Everyone who asks
will receive. Everyone who searches
will find. And the door will be opened
for everyone who knocks.

"Don't be frustrated by all you can't and don't understand now. In Heaven you will be continually learning and growing as a person. The day is coming when you will know and understand much more than you ever imagined possible. All of the various events of your life will finally make sense."

— Dave Earley, *The 21 Most Amazing Truths about Heaven*

In any serious discussion of the afterlife, one question inevitably—and understandably—arises.

How could a loving God send people to hell?

Many who argue against the concept of eternal damnation see the question as a verdict swayer—or, at the very least, an unsolvable conundrum. A loving God *wouldn't* send people to hell; therefore, hell does not exist.

Those who believe in a dual-destination eternity (heaven and hell) contend that the Bible addresses this question in detail, but its answer cannot be pinpointed to one specific verse. Rather, it starts with Genesis 1 and continues through Revelation 22. In every section of Scripture, we see aspects of God's nature and his interaction with humankind.

Each passage reveals a new clue—a piece of a jigsaw puzzle. Put them all together, and we get a three-dimensional (although somewhat limited) glimpse of God—one that helps us to better understand the less palatable aspects of theology.

It doesn't come easy. That sort of understanding takes time and effort. The question at hand is structured like an onion. In order to understand the surface topic of "hell as an eternal destination," we need to peel back a layer of biblical truth. In order to understand *that* truth, we need to dig a layer deeper—and then another, and another.

CHAPTER 4

THE PATH TO HEAVEN AND HELL

And let's be honest. Concepts in the Bible are infinite. There are only so many layers we can peel back before confusion may set in.

For purposes of this section, let's address the question by looking at the "onion" of biblical concepts as a cross section. We will start at the core and work our way out to discover how each concept is related.

We will explore

- God's plan for humankind;
- the impact of sin on God's plan;
- God's just nature;
- God's punishment for sin;
- the Old Testament system of sacrifice;
- the need for a perfect sacrifice;

- Jesus' victory over sin;
- Jesus' victory over death;
- Jesus' claim to be the only way to God;
- the Bible's promise to those who believe in Jesus;
- the hallmarks of heaven-bound people;
- the next steps in our understanding of the afterlife.

Our aim is not to persuade or change minds but to illuminate and give insight into the biblical basis of popular beliefs regarding heaven and hell.

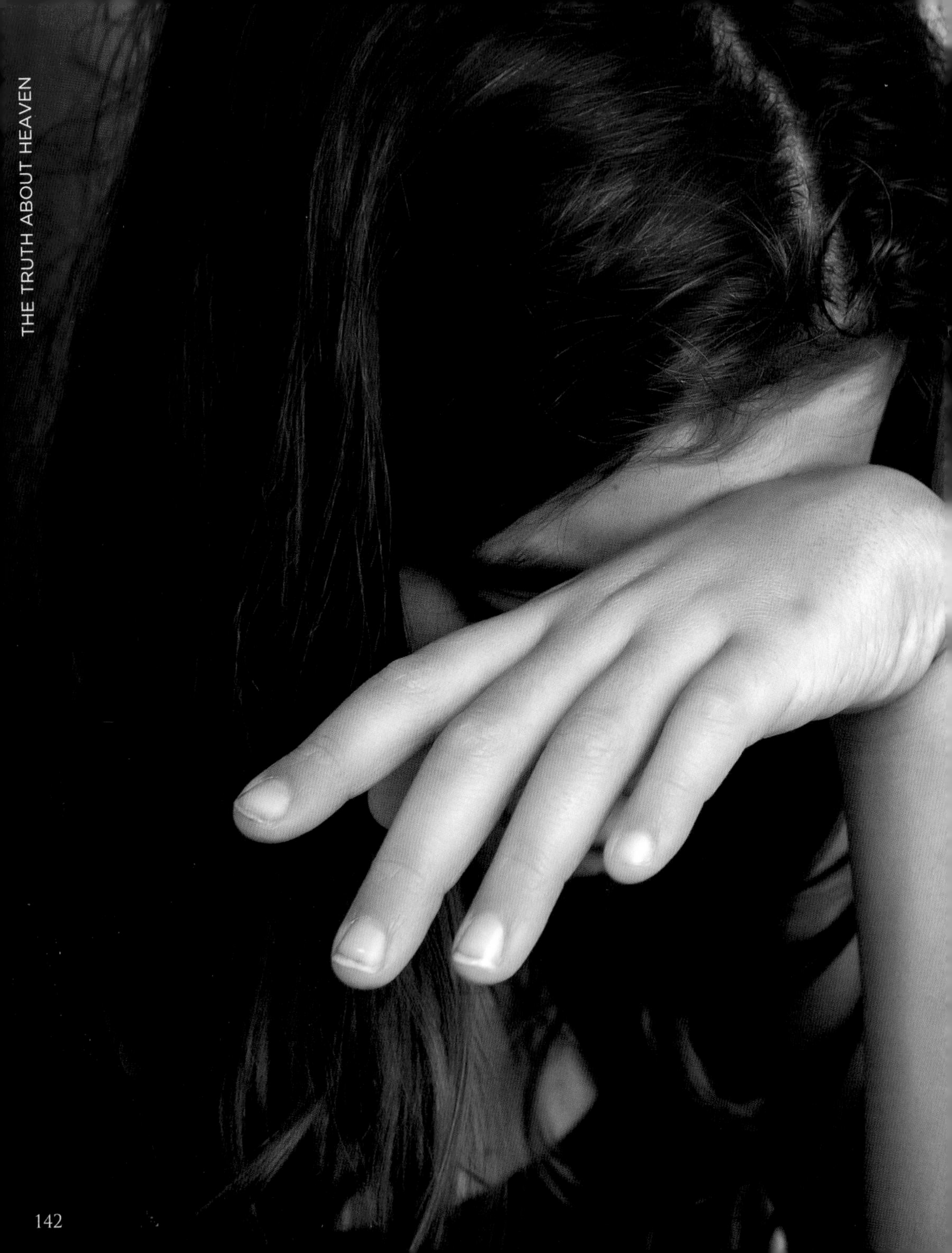

"Thinking seriously and biblically about hell is not something most people do. But Christians need to understand what God has saved them from, and unbelievers need to be warned of the eternal judgment that awaits them unless they repent of their sins and turn to Christ for salvation."

— Tony Evans, *Tony Evans Speaks Out on Heaven and Hell*

Read It for Yourself
GENESIS 2:8-14

The LORD made a garden in a place called Eden, which was in the east, and he put the man there. The LORD God filled the garden with all kinds of beautiful trees and fruit trees. Two other trees were in the middle of the garden. One of these gave life—the other gave the wisdom to know the difference between right and wrong. From Eden a river flowed out to water the garden, then it divided into four rivers. The first one is the Pishon River that flows through the land of Havilah, where pure gold, rare perfumes, and precious stones are found. The second is the Gihon River that winds through Ethiopia. The Tigris River that flows east of Assyria is the third, and the fourth is the Euphrates River.

GOD'S PLAN

What might have been.

These are the words that haunt every discussion of heaven and hell.

Our reality is that God has offered us a second chance—his perfect solution to the seemingly unsolvable problems that were caused by the sin of his own creation.

If we are going to ask a question that begins with the words "How could a loving God," the next words out of our mouths should be "do anything *more* for his human creation?"

God stacked the deck in humankind's favor. He gave us Eden—both a place *and* a spiritual condition. In a physical sense, Eden was a garden paradise—lush and teeming with life—a place so beautiful, so fruitful, so unspoiled that it has no modern-day equivalent. Eden was, in a spiritual sense, a place where all was right between God and humanity—where God could enjoy an intimate, unhindered relationship with man and woman. It is the place we have been trying to get back to ever since, whether we realize it or not.

The biblical narrative of life in the paradise of the Garden of Eden lasts only one chapter. But what a glorious picture is painted in that one chapter! We may not have the entire blueprint of God's plan, but we can see elements of it in Genesis 2.

Eden was a place of innocence.
Adam and Eve were naked: physically, emotionally, and spiritually. They had nothing to hide. Their interactions were marked with complete openness and transparency. No guilt. No shame. No remorse.

Eden was a place of perfect balance in nature.
God paraded all the animals past Adam so that the first man could give them names. This speaks of a harmony among creatures that no longer exists.

Eden was a place of fulfilling work.
God created Adam and Eve with a purpose. He designed them to find satisfaction in physical and mental effort. Adam and Eve were caretakers of paradise—and found real pleasure and joy in their responsibilities.

Eden was a place of intimate fellowship with God.
Genesis 3:8 describes God strolling through the garden in the cool of the evening. Adam and Eve were able to experience his presence in person, close enough to walk with him through the garden.

How could anyone possibly want more?

THE SPLIT

God could have compelled his human creation to love, obey, and worship him by force. He could have wired us in such a way that we would have no choice but to follow his will. But he wasn't interested in interacting with a race of automatons.

So he gave us free will—the freedom to choose to follow him as well as the freedom to choose not to follow him. His desire is for us to love, obey, and worship him because we recognize he is *worthy* of such honor—and, also, because we *want* to.

Obedience, of course, requires some kind of rule, warning, or stipulation—something to be obeyed. When God gave Eden to the human race, he told Adam and Eve they were free to eat from any tree in the garden—except one. The tree of the knowledge of good and evil was off-limits.

Humans had countless ways to honor God and enjoy the work of his creation. But they had only one way to disobey him—*one* rule.

One partially eaten fruit later, it was all over. Sin entered the human race. The results were devastating.

Sin brought an end to paradise.
Adam and Eve were expelled from the Garden of Eden and forbidden to return. They were forced to make their way in much more difficult and inhospitable surroundings.

Sin changed the natural world.
The harmony and mutual cooperation that marked interspecies life in Eden vanished. Beyond Eden's borders, the law of the jungle reigned supreme. It was every creature for itself.

Sin changed the nature of work.
Work no longer brought the same kind of pleasure and fulfillment it once did. Work became a chore, often a never-ending series of thankless, difficult tasks. In Eden, Adam and Eve were energized by their work. Outside Eden, they were drained and exhausted by it.

Sin opened a gulf between God and humans.
Because God is holy, sin cannot exist in his presence. Sin-stained people cannot enter, experience, or even survive in his presence. The intimacy Adam and Eve enjoyed with their Creator came to an end. Though the human race never stopped being objects of God's love, there were consequences for sin: humans also became objects of God's wrath.

In order for things to change—in order for humans to experience God's presence again—drastic measures had to be taken.

The Creation of the World and the Expulsion from Paradise, c. 1445
Giovanni di Paolo
(1395–1482)

Read It for Yourself
GENESIS 3:23-24

So the LORD God sent them out of the Garden of Eden, where they would have to work the ground from which the man had been made. Then God put winged creatures at the entrance to the garden and a flaming, flashing sword to guard the way to the life-giving tree.

"DEATH PREVENTS
US FROM STAYING
IN THIS SINFUL,
SUFFERING WORLD
OF SICKNESS."

— Paul P. Enns, *Heaven Revealed: What Is It Like? What Will We Do? . . .
And 11 Other Things You've Wondered About*

THE PROBLEM OF PERFECT JUSTICE

Grammatically speaking, "God is love" is a complete statement. It satisfies the requirements of a sentence because it contains both a noun and a verb—a subject and a predicate. However, theologically speaking, the statement is far from complete. It identifies just one of God's attributes.

Yes, God is love. But God is also

- independent (self-existent);
- omnipotent (all-powerful);
- unchangeable;
- eternal;
- omnipresent (not limited by space);
- spiritual;
- invisible;
- omniscient (all-knowing);
- wise;
- truthful;
- good;
- merciful;
- holy.

What's more, God is wrathful and just—two attributes that rarely get mentioned on Christian T-shirts or bumper stickers but that figure prominently in discussions of heaven and hell. The fact that God is wrathful means that he hates all sin. The fact that he is just means that he demands perfect punishment for sin.

Another key to the discussion of the afterlife is that God's attributes are in perfect unity and perfect balance. He is not partially loving and partially holy. He is perfectly loving, always; and he is perfectly holy, always. His attributes never contradict nor interfere with one another. God's mercifulness never occludes him from being holy—or vice versa.

To focus on one particular attribute, consider the question, "How could a loving God send someone to hell?" This accusation is a misunderstanding of God that reduces him to a one-dimensional caricature. We might as well ask, "How could a just God allow people who have sinned into heaven?"

God's justice and wrath cannot be "turned off" for the sake of his love. One attribute doesn't supersede another. God loves us and God must punish our sins are equally valid statements—and both are equally integral aspects of his relationship with us.

His plan to save us from punishment for our sin, thereby providing us a way to eternal life, had to satisfy all his attributes—perfectly.

Read It for Yourself
ACTS 17:30–31

In the past, God forgave all this because people did not know what they were doing. But now he says that everyone everywhere must turn to him. He has set a day when he will judge the world's people with fairness. And he has chosen the man Jesus to do the judging for him. God has given proof of this to all of us by raising Jesus from death.

God, the Creator of the universe, chose humans as the primary beneficiaries of his goodness and love. He gave us paradise. He gave us a mutually beneficial relationship with the world around us. He gave us a unique, satisfying, and ultimately fulfilling purpose for living. And, best of all, he gave us an intimate relationship with him.

In response—we, the human race, chose sin.

What is the proper punishment for so heinous a betrayal—for spitting in the eye of our Father, the Almighty? The question, in human terms, is moot. It couldn't be more moot, in fact. Our sin-clouded perspective prevents us from seeing the issue clearly. Our instinct for self-preservation and justification compels us to downplay the seriousness of our offense. Our delusions of grandeur convince us that somehow our "good works" cancel out our sins and make us fit for God's presence.

In short, our human limitations prevent us from rendering a just verdict. We can't see the matter from a perspective of holiness, so we have no say. Only One—who is perfectly holy and perfectly just—is qualified to accurately assess sin and determine the appropriate consequence. And that sentence has been on the books for millennia.

- *Sin pays off with death.* (Romans 6:23)
- *Then Jesus said, "Those people will be punished forever."* (Matthew 25:46)
- *Only those who sin will be put to death.* (Ezekiel 18:20)
- *When sin is finished with us, it leaves us dead.* (James 1:15)

God is the source of life. He invited us to enjoy that life in his presence forever, and we rejected it. In one sense, God gave us what we asked for when we chose to sin against him: existence apart from his presence.

In God's law book, the only just punishment for sin is spiritual death.

THE ONLY JUST PUNISHMENT

"It is impossible for a man to be freed from the habit of sin before he hates it, just as it is impossible to receive forgiveness before confessing his trespasses."

Ignatius

THE TRUTH ABOUT HEAVEN

It is only right for God to punish everyone who is causing you trouble, but he will give you relief from your troubles. God will do the same for us, when the Lord Jesus comes from heaven with his powerful angels and with a flaming fire.

Our Lord Jesus will punish anyone who doesn't know God and won't obey his message. Their punishment will be eternal destruction, and they will be kept far from the presence of our Lord and his glorious strength.

2 THESSALONIANS 1:6–9

The Damned Cast into Hell (detail), c. 1499–1504
Luca Signorelli (c. 1445–1523)

THE TEMPORARY SOLUTION

Daily Offerings at Solomon's Temple
Balage Balogh

Our rejection of God's plan did nothing to diminish his love for us. In his mercy, he reached out again with a second part of his plan—a covenant whereby the relationship between him and his people could be restored. The covenant requirements were drastic, but the severity of the circumstances made them necessary. God's people would learn that sin carries a brutal price.

The key to the covenant is found in Leviticus 17:11: *"Life is in the blood, and I have given you the blood of animals to sacrifice in place of your own."*

God required his people to make regular animal sacrifices to cover their sins—according to his specific guidelines, which are laid out in the Old Testament. God's sacrificial demands were exacting. Each sacrificed animal had to be spotless, without blemish, and as close to physically perfect as possible. Individuals would slaughter their animals and shed the animals' blood on altars. In so doing, they would acknowledge that the animals were being sacrificed in their stead.

Animal sacrifice plays a large role in Jewish biblical history. Abel, the son of Adam and Eve, pleased God by offering the firstborn from his flock. Noah built an altar and offered a sacrifice as the first act in the post-flood world. Moses and the Hebrew people offered sacrifices in the wilderness. Worship at the Jerusalem temple involved animal sacrifice.

Continual animal sacrifice was a way of life for God's people for one simple reason: one sacrifice was never enough. The blood of an animal, no matter how spotless, could never bring about perfect atonement. The best that God's people could hope for was to temporarily "cover" their sins—and to wait for God to provide the perfect sacrifice that would atone for the sins of the whole world, once and for all.

Read It for Yourself
HEBREWS 9:14

But Christ was sinless, and he offered himself as an eternal and spiritual sacrifice to God. This is why his blood is much more powerful and makes our consciences clear. Now we can serve the living God and no longer do things that lead to death.

157

Let's imagine the impossible. Let's say a person is born, lives a full life, and dies without violating any of God's commands. Let's say the person never utters a falsehood, never harbors a millisecond of ill will toward another person, and never gives God less than 100 percent devotion. Let's say the person's every thought, attitude, word, and deed honor God.

In the context of eternal life, such a sparkling résumé would still fall immeasurably short of the standard required for atoning for sin and restoring the relationship with God. Even if no sin were committed, the person would still have an inherited sinful nature to answer for. No one born of man and woman could offer the perfect sacrifice that God requires for the atonement of sin.

A person conceived by the Holy Spirit and delivered by a virgin, on the other hand, would have no inherited sinful nature. If that person could manage the impossible—live a sinless life with absolutely no offenses against God—he would be a fitting candidate to bring about atonement.

Of course, this perfect candidate would have to agree to endure unprecedented agony—the kind of torture and death that would be unimaginable to anyone else. This innocent, blameless specimen of perfection would be subjected to the totality of God's holy wrath and judgment for the sins of the world. The suffering and pain we deserve would instead be heaped on him. He who knew no sin would, in effect, *become* sin in God's eyes—and be punished accordingly.

Only One could satisfy those demands. But in order to do that, he had to leave his idyllic existence in heaven for a life of rejection, ridicule, and betrayal on our sin-ravaged planet. He had to give up his autonomy and become a helpless baby. He had to lay aside his perfections and make himself vulnerable to pain, sickness, and exhaustion. He had to submit to physical limitations, such as hunger and thirst. He had to squeeze his infinite presence into a container of flesh roughly five-and-a-half-feet tall.

Only Jesus could have bridged the gap between God and humanity. Only Jesus did.

Read It for Yourself
ISAIAH 9:6-7

A child has been born for us.
We have been given a son
   who will be our ruler.
His names will be
Wonderful Advisor
   and Mighty God,
Eternal Father
   and Prince of Peace.
His power will never end;
   peace will last forever.
He will rule David's kingdom
   and make it grow strong.
He will always rule
   with honesty and justice.
The Lord All-Powerful
will make certain
   that all of this is done.

The Adoration of the Shepherds, Giorgione (1470–1510)

THE PERFECT SACRIFICE

"Since we find it recorded in the memoirs of the apostles that he is the Son of God, and since we call him the Son, we have understood that he proceeded before all creatures from the Father by his power and his will . . . and that he became man by the virgin, in order that the disobedience which proceeded from the serpent might receive its destruction in the same way in which it derived its origin. For Eve, who was a virgin and undefiled, having conceived by the word of the serpent, brought forth disobedience and death. But the virgin Mary received faith and joy when the angel Gabriel announced the good news to her that the Spirit of the Lord would come upon her and the power of the Highest would overshadow her. Therefore, also, that which was begotten by her is the Son of God."

Justin Martyr, c. AD 150

GOD LOVED THE PEOPLE
OF THIS WORLD SO MUCH
THAT HE GAVE HIS ONLY SON,
SO THAT EVERYONE WHO
HAS FAITH IN HIM WILL HAVE
ETERNAL LIFE AND NEVER
REALLY DIE.

JOHN 3:16

THE CONQUERING OF SIN

The Temptation of Christ on the Mountain, 1308–1311
Duccio di Buoninsegna (1255–1319)

Jesus was fully God and fully human when he came to earth. He experienced the same kinds of urges and frustrations we experience. He faced the same opportunities to cut moral corners that we encounter.

Hebrews 4:15 says, *"Jesus understands every weakness of ours, because he was tempted in every way that we are. But he did not sin!"* Those words, true and lofty as they are, don't begin to describe what Jesus accomplished.

He went head-to-head with sin—on sin's home field and with sin at full strength. He had the eyes of heaven, and all of history, on *him*. His margin of error was nonexistent. Anything less than absolute perfection would have ended humanity's hope for eternal life. And there were plenty of opportunities for him to slip up.

According to Matthew 4, Jesus spent some time in the wilderness in preparation for his earthly ministry. He fasted for forty days and nights, which left him hungry, tired, and weak. His adversary, the devil, saw an opportunity and pounced. Just as he had done with Adam and Eve in the Garden of Eden, Satan tempted Jesus.

He urged Jesus to end the fast—to take care of his physical needs. He made Jesus an offer few would ever refuse. He quoted Scripture to support his points. He used his wiles to distract Jesus, to catch him off guard, to make him lose sight—even momentarily—of his mission. But the devil failed—miserably.

Jesus countered every temptation with a quote from God's Word. He never wavered, never slipped, and never gave anything less than a perfect answer. The devil went away, but the testing did not.

Wherever he traveled, Jesus faced relentless, intense scrutiny from the Jewish religious leaders. These men, arguably the most highly educated in all Israel, parsed Jesus' every word for misinterpretation, falsehood, or blasphemy. They laid political and religious traps for him, desperately trying to get him to say or do something wrong.

Jesus parried their every thrust. His answers to their accusations not only absolved him of any wrongdoing but also revealed important truths to his followers and exposed the religious leaders as petty hypocrites. Even the most devious minds in Israel could not cause him to sin.

When all their attempts failed, Jesus' enemies stacked the deck against him by coercing witnesses to lie about things he had said. They had him arrested and tortured. They mocked him as they beat him. Yet Jesus never once let his anger get the better of him.

He never gave up his sinlessness, his deity—his perfection. He went to his death as a spotless Lamb, the victor over sin.

THE CONQUERING OF DEATH

Jesus gave his life to pay humankind's penalty for sin. He satisfied God's demand for a perfect sacrifice. He destroyed the power of sin once and for all—and broke its grip on our lives.

Yet one obstacle still loomed large after Jesus' crucifixion. The apostle Paul explained it this way: *"Adam sinned, and that sin brought death into the world. Now everyone has sinned, and so everyone must die"* (Romans 5:12). We infected ourselves with mortality and then found we had no cure.

Death, for all intents and purposes, was an undefeated foe. When Jesus breathed his last breath on the cross, it must have appeared (to the untrained eye) that even *he* had succumbed to its power. *"Once again Jesus shouted, and then he died"* (Matthew 27:50). Several translations of this verse use the phrase "yielded up his spirit" to describe Jesus' final breath, which suggests a different balance of power. Death didn't *take* Jesus' life; Jesus *released his spirit*, willingly. Still, for one very long Sabbath, the eternal fate of humankind remained unchanged.

And then—Easter Sunday dawned.

The light of the new day revealed an open tomb, a pile of empty grave clothes, and an angel with a message for the ages: he is risen.

Jesus was alive. He took death's best shot, descended into the grave, and then emerged—victorious. The women at the tomb saw his resurrected body, as did his disciples and hundreds of other followers.

Every one of those witnesses could attest to the fact that Jesus had destroyed the power of the grave forever.

Jesus blazed the trail from death to eternal life. He knows the way, because he *is* the way. If we follow him, he will deliver us into his Father's presence when we die.

The bodies we now have are weak and can die. But they will be changed into bodies that are eternal. Then the Scriptures will come true,

> *"Death has lost the battle!*
> *Where is its victory?*
> *Where is its sting?"*
> (1 Corinthians 15:54–55)

"All God's plans have the mark of the cross on them, and all His plans have death to self in them."

E. M. Bounds

Christ's Side Pierced with a Lance, 1620
Peter Paul Rubens (1577–1640)

"[To have faith in Christ] means, of course, trying to do all that He says. There would be no sense in saying you trusted a person if you would not take his advice. Thus if you have really handed yourself over to Him, it must follow that you are trying to obey Him. But trying in a new way, a less worried way. Not doing these things in order to be saved, but because He has begun to save you already. Not hoping to get to Heaven as a reward for your actions, but inevitably wanting to act in a certain way because a first faint gleam of Heaven is already inside you."

— C. S. Lewis, *Mere Christianity*

THE CLAIM

Jesus made some audacious claims during his earthly ministry. He identified himself as the long-awaited Messiah, the Savior of God's chosen people whose coming had been foretold centuries earlier.

> The woman said, "I know that the Messiah will come. He is the one we call Christ. When he comes, he will explain everything to us."
>
> "I am that one," Jesus told her, "and I am speaking to you now." (John 4:25–26)

He identified himself as the Son of God.

> After Jesus had finished speaking to his disciples, he looked up toward heaven and prayed:
>
> Father, the time has come for you to bring glory to your Son, in order that he may bring glory to you. And you gave him power over all people . . . Now, Father, give me back the glory I had with you before the world was created. (John 17:1–5)

He identified himself as God: *"If you have seen me, you have seen the Father"* (John 14:9).

Even more audacious than his claims, though, was the evidence he offered to support them. He fulfilled the words of God's prophets. He displayed an unprecedented understanding of God's law. He enjoyed an intimate relationship with God the Father. He demonstrated a Creator's power over nature and the human condition.

In short, he left little doubt among his followers that he was who he claimed to be. That goes, also, for his most astounding claim of all: *"I am the way, the truth, and the life! . . . Without me, no one can go to the Father"* (John 14:6).

These words have eternal implications—namely, that apart from Jesus, we have no way of being reconciled with God or experiencing his presence. Without Christ, there is no eternal life.

Many people find such claims of exclusivity objectionable. In fact, to embrace Jesus' words in John 14:6 is to open one's self to accusations of being narrow-minded and intolerant. After all, if Jesus is the only way to God, where does that leave followers of other religions?

Christians counter those charges by pointing out the excruciating price Jesus paid. If there were an alternate route to God, one that didn't require his Son's perfect sacrifice, then Jesus' suffering and death were for naught.

The Tribute Money, c. 1625
Anthony van Dyck (1599–1641)

JOHN 14:1-14

Jesus said to his disciples, "Don't be worried! Have faith in God and have faith in me. There are many rooms in my Father's house. I wouldn't tell you this, unless it was true. I am going there to prepare a place for each of you. After I have done this, I will come back and take you with me. Then we will be together. You know the way to where I am going."

Thomas said, "Lord, we don't even know where you are going! How can we know the way?"

"I am the way, the truth, and the life!" Jesus answered. "Without me, no one can go to the Father. If you had really known me, you would have known the Father. But from now on, you do know him, and you have seen him."

Philip said, "Lord, show us the Father. That is all we need."

Jesus replied:

"Philip, I have been with you for a long time. Don't you know who I am? If you have seen me, you have seen the Father. How can you ask me to show you the Father? Don't you believe that I am one with the Father and that the Father is one with me? What I say isn't said on my own. The Father who lives in me does these things.

"Have faith in me when I say that the Father is one with me and that I am one with the Father. Or else have faith in me simply because of the things I do. I tell you for certain that if you have faith in me, you will do the same things I am doing. You will do even greater things, now that I am going back to the Father. Ask me, and I will do whatever you ask. This way the Son will bring honor to the Father. I will do whatever you ask me to do."

THE PROMISE

John 3:16 has become a staple of the Christian faith (not to mention a favorite of sign-waving football fans) for a reason. Few other Bible verses summarize the promise of heaven as succinctly as it does: *"God loved the people of this world so much that he gave his only Son, so that everyone who has faith in him will have eternal life and never really die."* The equation that opens heaven to the human race is established in this verse:

Belief in Jesus = Eternal Life

Jesus reinforced the validity of this equation during his crucifixion. One of the criminals executed with him recognized Jesus as the Messiah. Details about this encounter are scarce, but somehow the man understood that Jesus held the keys to the hereafter.

"Then he said to Jesus, 'Remember me when you come into power!' Jesus replied, 'I promise that today you will be with me in paradise' " (Luke 23:42–43). The man expressed his belief in Jesus and received immediate assurance of eternal life from the Lord himself.

Years later, the apostle Paul and his traveling companion Silas were imprisoned in Philippi for preaching and healing in Jesus' name. One night, an earthquake opened all the cell doors of the prison. The jailer naturally assumed all the prisoners had escaped. Realizing that he would be held responsible for the security breach, the jailer pulled out his sword to kill himself.

But Paul shouted, "Don't harm yourself! No one has escaped."

The jailer asked for a torch and went into the jail. He was shaking all over as he knelt down in front of Paul and Silas. After he had led them out of the jail, he asked, "What must I do to be saved?"

They replied, "Have faith in the Lord Jesus and you will be saved!" (Acts 16:28–31)

There is no magic incantation, no password to get into heaven. Eternal life is given to everyone who takes Jesus at his word, everyone who believes that Jesus' death and resurrection make heaven a reality, everyone who believes that eternal life in God's presence is possible only through Jesus.

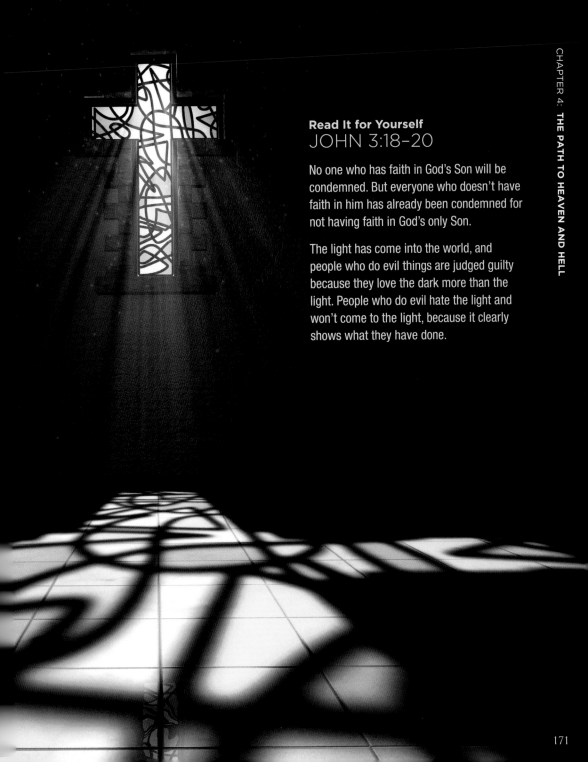

Read It for Yourself
JOHN 3:18–20

No one who has faith in God's Son will be condemned. But everyone who doesn't have faith in him has already been condemned for not having faith in God's only Son.

The light has come into the world, and people who do evil things are judged guilty because they love the dark more than the light. People who do evil hate the light and won't come to the light, because it clearly shows what they have done.

THE HALLMARKS OF THE HEAVEN BOUND

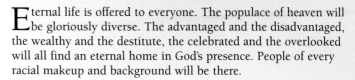

Eternal life is offered to everyone. The populace of heaven will be gloriously diverse. The advantaged and the disadvantaged, the wealthy and the destitute, the celebrated and the overlooked will all find an eternal home in God's presence. People of every racial makeup and background will be there.

Yet for all that diversity, there are a few characteristics that all heaven-bound people share—or should share.

A Grateful Heart

"Be thankful and praise the LORD *as you enter his temple"*
(Psalm 100:4).

Our heavenly Father reached out to us after we rejected him and—at an unimaginable cost to himself—provided a way for us to experience eternity in his presence. Why should we wait for heaven to show our thankfulness?

A Humble Spirit

"You were saved by faith in God, who treats us much better than we deserve. This is God's gift to you, and not anything you have done on your own. It isn't something you have earned, so there is nothing you can brag about" (Ephesians 2:8–9).

To put our faith in Jesus for salvation and eternal life is to acknowledge that we did nothing to deserve either. Our heaven-bound status doesn't mean that we're "morally superior." We are simply recipients of the greatest gift ever, and our attitude should reflect that.

An Attraction to God's Word

"Instead, they find happiness in the Teaching of the LORD, *and they think about it day and night"* (Psalm 1:2).

When we study the Bible—when we think about or meditate on God's words—we draw closer to him. We enter his presence. We experience a taste of his glory here on earth and a sneak preview of what's to come.

A Concern for Others

"When all your people met, I did not keep silent. I said, 'Our LORD *is kind. He is faithful and caring, and he saves us' "* (Psalm 40:10).

Good news is for sharing. The good news of Jesus is for sharing with everyone.

WHERE DO WE GO FROM HERE?

Though the Bible is vague on certain details of the afterlife, there is one point on which it is quite specific: believing in Jesus is a starting point, not a finish line. How you proceed from there is up to you. Whatever you choose to do, though, make sure you're covered in three general areas:

Know what you believe.
"Your word is a lamp that gives light wherever I walk" (Psalm 119:105).

Whether you're looking for illumination on this life or the next, you'll find it in God's Word. The Bible is our primary source of information about God, his interaction with humanity, his will, and his plan for the future. The more time you spend in Scripture, the better acquainted you'll become with him—and the deeper your relationship will grow.

If you don't know where to begin, choose a specific topic to explore. Take heaven, for example. Study every passage you can find about heaven, what it's like, and how to get there. Learn what the Bible says—and *doesn't* say—about the afterlife.

Don't let the Bible's size and reputation intimidate you. Remember this: God takes a special delight in people who delve into his Word, and he offers divine assistance—through his Spirit and fellow believers—to those who are seeking to understand it.

Know why you believe.
"Keep on being faithful to what you were taught and to what you believed. After all, you know who taught you these things. Since childhood, you have known the Holy Scriptures that are able to make you wise enough to have faith in Christ Jesus and be saved. Everything in the Scriptures is God's Word. All of it is useful for teaching and helping people and for correcting them and showing them how to live. The Scriptures train God's servants to do all kinds of good deeds" (2 Timothy 3:14–17).

Not everything you read in Scripture will make sense—at *first*. Some passages will confuse you. Some will confound your expectations. Some will raise troubling questions. That's when the assistance of a trustworthy Christian leader or mature believer can make all the difference in the world.

A spiritually mature believer can help you

- find answers to your nagging questions;
- work through your doubts;
- make connections between passages of Scripture;
- understand the Holy Spirit's role in providing believers with understanding;
- recognize the implications of certain Bible teachings;
- find ways to apply what you learn to your daily life.

If you're in need of such a person, talk to your pastor, Sunday school teacher, small group leader, or a respected member of your church. If, on the other hand, you are a mature believer, look for ways to assist young or struggling Christians.

Know how to communicate what you believe—and why.
"Always be ready to give an answer when someone asks you about your hope"
(1 Peter 3:15b).

The more secure you are in your knowledge of Scripture (the more you know what the Bible says about any given topic), the more comfortable you'll be when you talk to others about it. Conversely, the more experience you gain by talking to others, the better equipped you'll be to

- anticipate and answer certain frequently asked questions;
- defuse loaded or controversial topics;
- offer reasonable and effective responses to people's objections;
- communicate your beliefs in a way that resonates with individuals.

"This is the greatest gift God can give you: to understand what happened in your life. To have it explained. It is the peace you have been searching for."

— Mitch Albom, *The Five People You Meet in Heaven*

Nobody will ever accuse God of spoon-feeding his people. His Word is not a pamphlet with the "stuff we need to know" highlighted for us. It's a sprawling, complicated, challenging work that requires careful reading and thoughtful application.

When Jesus came to earth, he didn't speak in bullet points; he spoke in parables. He confused and frustrated most of his listeners. He answered questions with questions. He demanded that his followers think critically.

It comes as no surprise, therefore, that certain aspects of eternity challenge us in Scripture. You might say the Bible raises more questions about heaven and hell than it answers! God allows us to come up with our own conclusions, theories, and conjectures based on what we know about his nature, his work, and his will.

The questions addressed in this section fall squarely into that "difficult" category:

- Will there be animals in heaven?
- What age will we be in heaven?
- Will we know everything in heaven?
- Will people in heaven be aware of what's happening on earth?
- Will we be bored in heaven?
- Should we believe people who claim to have seen heaven?

Some of these questions may seem trivial to you; and others may seem vital. Yet all of them add something to our understanding of and attitude toward God's plan for our eternity. As such, they're worthy of our consideration.

Clear-cut answers may be hard to come by, but educated guesses are not. After all, we have God-given intellect, as well as some helpful clues tucked away in his Word, to guide us. We also have a heavenly Father who rewards those who prayerfully seek him, his Word, and his will.

What more could we ask for?

CHAPTER 5
HEAVENLY QUESTIONS

WILL HEAVEN BE PET-FRIENDLY?

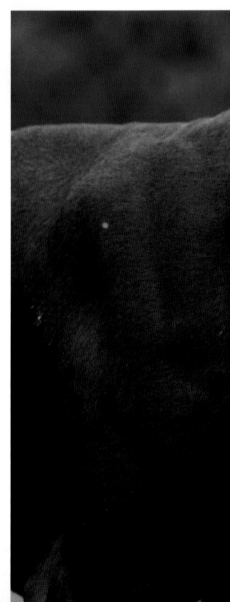

Heaven presents a real dilemma for some pet owners. They cannot fathom eternity apart from their beloved Shih Tzu, Persian, macaw, or Vietnamese pot-bellied pig.

Their adoration is best summarized by the meme that shows an adorable dog next to the caption, "Some of the people waiting for you in heaven are not people at all."

So, is that theological fact or wishful thinking? Do animals go to heaven?

Let's approach the question from a redemptive perspective. The Bible makes no mention of animals having souls—or being included in God's plan of salvation. Some people claim that animal souls are different from human souls and that animals don't need to be redeemed.

Famed Christian writer C. S. Lewis suggested that a pet's ticket into heaven may be contingent upon the salvation of its owner. But that's just pure speculation.

We can also approach the question from animals' roles in creation. Animals played a significant role in God's original creation. Therefore it stands to reason that God will feature them prominently in his new creation (as described in Revelation 21–22).

Other biblical passages specifically mention animals with respect to the heavenly landscape. Isaiah 65:25 refers to wolves, lambs, lions, oxen, and snakes. Revelation 19:14 mentions horses. Surely the heavenly menagerie is more extensive than we can imagine!

C. S. Lewis suggested, acknowledging that he was going out on a theological limb, that animals "attain a real **self** in their masters in a sense similar to the way humans attain real life **in** Christ. And in this sense, it seems . . . that certain animals may have an immortality, not in themselves, but in the immortality of their masters."

WILL I LOOK YOUNG AGAIN ONCE IN HEAVEN?

Age is a funny thing. We spend most of our youth trying to look older than we really are and most of our later years trying to look younger. So where's the happy medium? What's the ideal age?

On earth, that question has only temporary significance. In heaven, its implications are eternal. If we're going to live forever, what age will we be? Will we remain the same age as we were at the time of our death? Will children who die in infancy be infants in heaven? Will people who die of old age be elderly for eternity? If so, doesn't that alter our opinion of heaven, at least a little?

The Bible is silent on the matter, but Bible scholars aren't. Some believe our heavenly bodies will be set to an "ideal age." This means that deceased infants would be advanced to a certain age. Those who die as senior citizens would have their body clocks set back.

Some people would choose 18 as the ideal age for heavenly citizens. Others would choose 21, or 25, or 30—or whatever age they consider their prime. As with other questions in this section, wishful thinking plays a large role in how we respond.

Centuries ago, Bible scholars claimed that everyone in heaven will be thirty-three years old—Jesus' age at the time of his death. They used the apostle John's words in 1 John 3:2 to support their claim: *"My dear friends, we are already God's children, though what we will be hasn't yet been seen. But we do know when Christ returns, we will be like him, because we will see him as he truly is."* They believed that being "like" Jesus in the afterlife also meant being his age.

Perhaps our best approach to this topic is to fall back on an old cliché: *Age is just a number.*

Our bodies, after all, will be renewed. No longer will we be subject to pain, sickness, or death. So in that sense we will be the perfect age, in perfect health, and in perfect condition.

"Ignorance is the curse of God; knowledge
is the wing wherewith we fly to heaven."

William Shakespeare

WILL WE KNOW EVERYTHING?

The apostle Paul served up a tantalizing possibility in 1 Corinthians 13:12: *"Now all we can see of God is like a cloudy picture in a mirror. Later we will see him face to face. We don't know everything, but then we will, just as God completely understands us."*

Everything? Completely? Seriously? Is Paul saying we can expect to become all-knowing in heaven?

Most Bible scholars would say no. From Paul's words they conclude that in heaven we will know as much as we're capable of knowing. That is, unimaginably more than we know now, but unimaginably less than God knows. Those scholars would hasten to add that only God is omniscient (all-knowing).

Let's add that to the list of things to thank him for when we enter his presence!

Omniscience, in the wrong hands, would feel more like an eternal punishment than a heavenly reward. Imagine the boredom of having nothing left to discover, nothing left to learn, and no hope of ever being surprised. Only one who is omnipotent (all-powerful) would have the wherewithal to endure being omniscient.

Mark 13:32 makes it clear that the angels in heaven aren't all-knowing. There is certain information that they're not privy to. If they don't know everything, there's no reason to believe we will.

What we will enjoy in heaven is the endless capacity to learn. Imagine being able to ask any question that you've ever pondered—and then receiving answers that fully satisfy your curiosity. Imagine spending eternity exploring the depths of God, knowing you'll never come close to comprehending him, and taking extraordinary delight in your efforts to do so.

CAN PEOPLE IN HEAVEN SEE WHAT'S HAPPENING ON EARTH?

No matter how strong or spiritually well-adjusted we think we are, the loss of a loved one can leave us "grasping at straws"—searching for nuggets of spiritual comfort to help ease the pain. One of the most popular "straws" is the idea that our deceased loved ones assume the role of spiritual protectors and advisors when they get to heaven. That is, they watch over us to ensure that we stay safe and make wise decisions. Some people take that concept to the extreme, suggesting that the dearly departed become guardian angels for their living loved ones.

The problem with these "straws of spiritual comfort" is that they're not based on biblical teachings. The Bible offers no definitive discussion about relatives serving as guardian angels, although it does draw a clear distinction between humans and angels (which shoots down the possibility of crossover between the two).

So we're left with this question: Do people in heaven know—and care—about what's happening here on earth?

In Luke 16 we read the story of a rich man who died and whose soul went to hell (verse 23). Even in his torment, the man was still concerned about his unbelieving brothers. He didn't want them to suffer his eternal fate. So, if we take the story at face value, we may conclude that in the afterlife we retain memories of our time on earth.

Regarding the more pleasant eternal destination, Jesus said, *"There is more happiness in heaven because of one sinner who turns to God than over 99 good people who don't need to"* (Luke 15:7). From this statement we may conclude that people in heaven are not only aware of earthly events but they actually have a profound interest in them.

But how far does that interest extend?

If the people in heaven are overly interested in earthly doings, it doesn't speak well of our eternal home. At some level, most of us would prefer to be so overwhelmed by the perfection of heaven that we will have little need to preoccupy ourselves with the rampant imperfection on earth.

WILL HEAVEN FEEL LIKE AN ETERNAL CHURCH SERVICE?

If you've spent any time in a thriving church, then some of the worship and fellowship scenes in the apostle John's vision of heaven may seem familiar to you.

For better or worse.

Think of the last time your congregation was especially fired up on a Sunday morning and belted out a song of praise that not only stirred your soul but also gave you goose bumps. Multiply that experience by infinity, and you get a rough approximation of what heavenly worship is like, according to Scripture.

On the flip side . . .

Think about the last time a Sunday morning service ran long—or seemed to. Recall that antsy feeling, that restlessness, that painful sensation of time passing by ever so slowly. Multiply that experience by infinity, and you get a rough approximation of the secret fear many people share about heaven.

The Bible's descriptions of the afterlife are awe-inspiring, but they fail to answer one very important question: Will we be bored in heaven?

That sound you hear right now is hundreds of thousands of pastors, Sunday school teachers, and Bible scholars rising together as one to offer an emphatic NO! But can we trust their opinion? What if they have a much higher tolerance for long worship services than we do?

One source that can be trusted is God's Word. And while there are no passages that explicitly guarantee that our interest will remain piqued for eternity, we do find indications in God's Word that we can look forward to an infinitely exciting heaven. God said these words to Jeremiah: *"Jeremiah, I am your Creator, and before you were born, I chose you to speak for me to the nations"* (Jeremiah 1:5).

God knows us. He always has. He knows what interests us. He knows what inspires us. He knows what gives us joy, contentment, and fulfillment.

He knows those things because he formed us before we were born. We are the way we are because God created us that way. Why, then, would we ever doubt that he will use that knowledge to make heaven eternally fresh, eternally fulfilling, and eternally exciting for us?

Does this sound familiar? "I saw a bright light."

The accounts of people who claim to have died and gone to heaven, albeit temporarily, differ in their circumstances, descriptions, and conclusions. Yet one detail remains a near constant: an overwhelming majority of these people mention a bright light—a heavenly "glow." So the question is raised: Should we add "quality lighting" to the list of things that are known about heaven?

More to the point, should we believe the stories of people who claim to have seen heaven?

Heaven Is for Real; Proof of Heaven; To Heaven and Back . . . The list goes on. You've heard of the books—perhaps even read one or two of them. And who can blame the authors or publishers for producing these works? Heaven is what believers live for. It is our hope eternal. So if someone claims to have an inside track on the topic, of course our curiosity will be piqued.

How exactly are we to respond to these fantastic accounts?

Reject the ones that contradict Scripture.
In order to spot counterfeits, we need to familiarize ourselves with the real deal. That is, we need to study the book of Revelation and other Bible passages that deal with the hereafter. The more we know of what God's Word says about heaven, the better equipped we will be to recognize—and reject—false stories.

Take the ones that are extrabiblical with a grain of salt.
Some accounts may not contradict Scripture, per se; but they don't necessarily track with Scripture, either. They offer details that go beyond what the Bible says. Those claims should be met with a healthy dose of skepticism.

Look first for a profit motive behind the story.
Does the person stand to gain financially as a result of the account? Is the person looking for publicity or notoriety? If the answer is yes, don't be too quick to believe the story.

Pray about the ones that seem biblical.
Ask God to give you discernment to help you determine what is and isn't real when it comes to heaven.

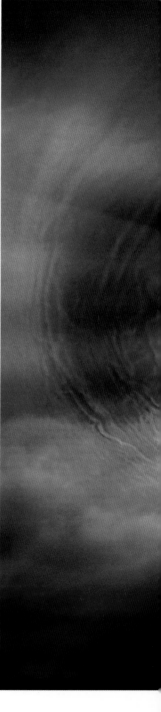

ARE NEAR-DEATH EXPERIENCES LEGITIMATE?

Read It for Yourself
PHILIPPIANS 3:20–21

But we are citizens of heaven and are eagerly waiting for our Savior to come from there. Our Lord Jesus Christ has power over everything, and he will make these poor bodies of ours like his own glorious body.

we talk about heaven being so far away. It is within speaking distance to those who belong there. Heaven is a prepared place for a prepared people."

— D. L. Moody